Praise for *WHAT IF THIS IS HEAVEN?*

"So many people have such a fear of death that they are afraid to live life to its fullest measure. Anita Moorjani does a brilliant job of demystifying both life and death by first breaking the spell of our conditioned beliefs and then giving us the practical tools to be reborn in the same life. This book will free your soul and teach you that you don't have to die to go to heaven."

— **Dr Joe Dispenza**, *New York Times* bestselling author of *You Are the Placebo*

"The richest literature on near-death experiences moves beyond mere descriptions of the afterlife. The greatest lessons concern how to live this life to the fullest. In her newest book, What if This is Heaven?*, Anita Moorjani addresses deeply held misconceptions in our modern global culture. Her evolving wisdom empowers readers toward much greater health and harmony: to truly love oneself in the face of life's challenges is integral to every human's fulfillment here on earth."*

— **Dr Eben Alexander**, neurosurgeon and author of *Proof of Heaven* and *The Map of Heaven*

What if
This is
Heaven?

ALSO BY ANITA MOORJANI

DYING TO BE ME:
My Journey from Cancer, to Near Death, to True Healing

The above may be ordered by visiting:

Hay House UK: www.hayhouse.co.uk
Hay House USA: www.hayhouse.com®
Hay House Australia: www.hayhouse.com.au
Hay House India: www.hayhouse.co.in

What if This is Heaven?

How I Released My Limiting Beliefs and Really Started Living

ANITA MOORJANI

HAY HOUSE

Carlsbad, California • New York City • London
Sydney •Johannesburg • Vancouver • New Delhi

First published and distributed in the United Kingdom by:
Hay House UK Ltd, Astley House, 33 Notting Hill Gate, London W11 3JQ
Tel: +44 (0)20 3675 2450; Fax: +44 (0)20 3675 2451; www.hayhouse.co.uk

Published and distributed in the United States of America by:
Hay House Inc., PO Box 5100, Carlsbad, CA 92018-5100
Tel: (1) 760 431 7695 or (800) 654 5126
Fax: (1) 760 431 6948 or (800) 650 5115; www.hayhouse.com

Published and distributed in Australia by:
Hay House Australia Ltd, 18/36 Ralph St, Alexandria NSW 2015
Tel: (61) 2 9669 4299; Fax: (61) 2 9669 4144; www.hayhouse.com.au

Published and distributed in the Republic of South Africa by:
Hay House SA (Pty) Ltd, PO Box 990, Witkoppen 2068
info@hayhouse.co.za; www.hayhouse.co.za

Published and distributed in India by:
Hay House Publishers India, Muskaan Complex, Plot No.3, B-2,
Vasant Kunj, New Delhi 110 070
Tel: (91) 11 4176 1620; Fax: (91) 11 4176 1630; www.hayhouse.co.in

Distributed in Canada by:
Raincoast Books, 2440 Viking Way, Richmond, B.C. V6V 1N2
Tel: (1) 604 448 7100; Fax: (1) 604 270 7161; www.raincoast.com

Cover design: Amy Rose Grigoriou and Leanne Siu Anastasi
Interior design: Riann Bender

The information given in this book should not be treated as a substitute for professional medical advice; always consult a medical practitioner. Any use of information in this book is at the reader's discretion and risk. Neither the author nor the publisher can be held responsible for any loss, claim or damage arising out of the use, or misuse, of the suggestions made, the failure to take medical advice or for any material on third party websites.

Author's note: Some of the stories that appear in this book are composites; individual names and identifying characteristics may have been changed for privacy reasons. Some conversations have been combined to present a more comprehensive treatment of the subject. Nevertheless, these stories reflect authentic discussions I've had with many readers and workshop participants over the years.

A catalogue record for this book is available from the British Library.

ISBN: 978-1-78180-199-4

Printed and bound in Great Britain by TJ International Ltd, Padstow, Cornwall.

In Memory of Wayne Dyer

Thank you, Wayne, for not dying with your music still in you. We continue to hear your song within the silence of our hearts. Yours was a life that will touch other lives forever. You, my friend, will live for eternity.

CONTENTS

When I was born into this world
The only things I knew were to love, laugh, and shine my light brightly.
Then as I grew, people told me to stop laughing.
"Take life seriously," they said,
"If you want to get ahead in this world."
So I stopped laughing.
People told me, "Be careful who you love
If you don't want your heart broken."
So I stopped loving.
They said, "Don't shine your light so bright
As it draws too much attention onto you."
So I stopped shining
And became small
And withered
And died
Only to learn upon death
That all that matters in life
Is to love, laugh, and shine our light brightly!

—ANITA MOORJANI

INTRODUCTION

What if you were suddenly to realize that *this* is heaven (or nirvana)—this physical life we are living right now? I know it sounds crazy, and I can sense some of you thinking, *If this is heaven, then why does it feel like hell to me?* And I hear you. It sure felt like that to me when I was being bullied as a child, taunted and discriminated against for the color of my skin and my family origin—things I had no control over. And it certainly felt like hell again when I was going through cancer, being in constant pain and fear for all those years.

But play along with me for a bit.

What if the reason my life felt like hell all that time was because I didn't know how powerful I was, or what I was capable of doing? After all, no one ever taught me how life worked, and we aren't born with an instruction manual. Life truly was a struggle for me, and I lived in immense fear well into adulthood. I believed that life happens *to* us and that I was a victim, so I was always reacting to my life circumstances instead of creating them. Who would create a childhood of bullying and discrimination that would leave her with such horrible low self-esteem? Who would choose to be born as a woman into a culture that still believes women are inferior to men? Who would create cancer in her own body—cancer that would nearly kill her? Of *course* I was a victim of my circumstances, or so I thought—until I died.

Much of my life story is chronicled in my first book, *Dying to Be Me*. Best-selling author and speaker Dr. Wayne Dyer was the one who brought my story into the public arena and encouraged me to write that book. Until his death just a few months ago, he continued to encourage his audiences to turn to my work. I know that his involvement in my life's purpose was divinely orchestrated as part of the unfolding of the greater tapestry. I am truly grateful for and humbled by what has transpired in my life as a result of what this amazing man has done for me.

When I wrote that first book, I never expected to write a second one. *I have written my memoir,* I thought, *which narrated my life and especially my experience with cancer, culminating in a near-death experience (NDE). And I've also written about the wisdom I gained from the whole experience. What more is there to write?* I really thought all the interesting elements in my life were already recounted in that book.

But one of the most striking insights my NDE gave me was that this life—the life we are all living now on earth—could become a heaven for us if we simply understood how it worked and what we needed to do to create that heaven as our reality. A major reason why I chose to return to this life during my NDE was because I understood that heaven is a state and *not* a place, and I wanted to experience, firsthand, the heaven that this life could actually be. I wanted to live out the amazing truth of this reality and transform the life of fear and dread and heartache that I had previously experienced. I wanted to live in heaven *here* . . . and *now*.

A Bumpy Reintegration

When I was in the NDE state, this all seemed so clear, so easy. But as I tried to integrate my newly realized insights and apply them to my life after my NDE, I kept running into roadblocks, particularly when I tried to connect or interact with other people. My view of what constitutes reality had changed dramatically, and it simply didn't fit in with what most people considered a normal worldview.

In an effort to feel as if I belonged in society once more, I would find myself trying to appease those who were disapproving of me. And if I didn't catch myself, I would start to suppress who I was or compromise much of what I had learned from my sojourn into the other realm in an effort to win approval. Whenever that happened, I'd start to feel disempowered again. Those amazing feelings of being invincible and being the creator of my life would erode, and old thought patterns and behaviors would start to creep in and cloud my vision. Fears of not "doing what's right" or concerns of disappointing others would resurface when I chose to pander to the critics, dancing to their tune instead of listening to my heart. (I'm sure many others can relate to this as well!) New anxieties took over, and before long I started to feel lost and abandoned. It seemed I was always choosing between fitting in or creating heaven.

At the same time, because of the celebrity that *Dying to Be Me* brought me, I began receiving an avalanche of letters and e-mails from people who were touched by my testimony. Many of these messages made me cry tears of joy and gratitude, and many people felt I was telling their story! It seemed to them that I had read their hearts, their minds, and their souls.

This overwhelming response was so unexpected. I had no idea my story would touch so many people at such a deep level. I was also blessed with numerous speaking invitations, both live public presentations as well as radio and television interviews. And after each engagement, people wanted more! They had many questions and wanted to delve further into my story—and theirs. Many were dealing with illnesses or had loved ones who were suffering or dying, while others were struggling in relationships or had money issues. Through all these life challenges, they wanted to learn more about bringing that piece of heaven I had experienced into their own lives here on earth.

Although the public response to my book was overwhelmingly positive, all the focused attention brought me to a new and deeper level of awareness within my own life journey, and it was becoming more and more important to me to spend time alone when I was not in the public arena. Whenever I was alone, I would still my thoughts and take myself back to the state I had experienced during my NDE, the state of being pure consciousness and realizing that we are all connected. In that state I could *feel* what everyone else was feeling as though it were my own emotion, including the sorrow and pain my family felt at the prospect of losing me. But it wasn't just my family's pain I was experiencing now. I could feel the pain of the whole world in my heart from reading all the stories that people would share with me.

They wanted me to come to their town, their church, their ashram, their home. They wanted to talk to me. I wanted to help them all, and it hurt me that I couldn't! No matter how many people I spoke to, how many letters I answered, it was never enough. There were always more that I couldn't respond to. I was feeling both people's suffering and, at the same time, my own pain for not being able to help them all. At times it was overwhelming. Slowly, my own joy started to ebb, and I knew I couldn't continue this way. My book had been intended to show people how to bring joy into their life, but how could I possibly bring joy into the world if I was mostly feeling everyone else's pain?

A New Opportunity to Heal

Then one day I took myself to my favorite place—the beach by my home—and I sat on the sand and looked out at the sea that separated the island where I lived in Hong Kong from the mainland. It was a cloudy day, so the sun was hiding. I'd come to this place because whenever I was feeling troubled, I would immerse myself in nature. In nature, particularly near the sea, I could physically *feel* the incredible connection we all have with the whole universe, as though everything was harmoniously working together in synchronization to form this vast tapestry we call life. No matter what my questions were, I always felt that answers came to me whenever I was in nature, whether those answers came through the whispers of the wind, the sound of the water, or the rustle of the tree branches and leaves. So as I sat there on the sand that day, looking out toward the sea and the sky, I spoke silently to the universe.

"I came back from death," I said. "Now what? This is heart-breaking for me. How am I supposed to be of help to all these people—and to myself—from the perspective of my puny physical being? If I had stayed in the NDE realm, maybe I could have helped a greater number of people. But all I feel is heartache for every person I can't help!"

Tears streamed down my face as I surrendered to the universe, questioning why I had come back. Why was I having to endure this heartache? And why *was* our world filled with so much of that pain?

Then, out of nowhere, I heard a whisper—not a real voice, but one that seemed to come from the sound of the waves in the sea, a sound that resonated in my heart. "What was the main message you learned from your near-death experience," the whisper asked, "the message you wrote about in your first book?"

"To love myself unconditionally," I answered. "And to be as much myself as I can be. To shine my light as brightly as I can."

"And that is all you need to do or be. Nothing more. Just love yourself unconditionally, always, and be who you are."

"But we live in a world that does not support thinking or feeling this way. It's as though this world is much more a hell than a heaven," I challenged the invisible voice as I watched the waves crashing against the rocks at the far end of the beach. "People all around me are facing so many challenges every day, and I don't know how I can help them by loving myself!"

"When you love yourself and know your true worth, there is nothing you cannot do or heal. You yourself learned this when you defied all medical knowledge and healed end-stage cancer. The cancer healed when you became aware of your worth."

This was absolutely true. Until I got lymphoma, I had lived a life filled with fear, but learning to love myself saved my life. It sounded so simple, yet why was it so difficult to convey this to others who were struggling? And why had it been so easy for me to lose this understanding once I attained it?

"It's easy to lose that knowledge of our true power when we are surrounded by people who don't believe in it or have never experienced it—which often may seem like most of the people in this world," I heard the voice answer, as if it had read my thoughts. "And if you continue to focus on how everyone else is feeling and what everyone else is wanting, you will get lost in the world of fear once more—and that is certainly not something you want to do again.

"Remember, your only work is to love yourself, value yourself, and embody this truth of self-worth and self-love so that you can be love in action. That is true service, to yourself and to those who surround you. Realizing how loved and valued you are is what healed your cancer. This same knowledge is what will help you to create a life of heaven here on earth. You are serving no one when you get lost in the problems of the world. So the only question you need to ask yourself when you are feeling defeated or lost is, *Where am I not loving myself? How can I value myself more?*"

Although this was exactly what I had learned in my NDE, and it was indeed what had healed me, it seemed that I had forgotten. I had lost myself in everyone else's pain, and now I was dumbstruck by the intensity of what had just happened. In that moment, I felt as though I held the answer to every question I had ever asked. What the whispering of the waves had shared with me was so simple, and yet so profound!

This experience also clearly revealed how easy it is for us to lose focus on our true purpose and to get caught up in the web of dramas we weave in order to justify our existence. I now understood that this is what happens to us once we immerse ourselves in the dominant beliefs of our surrounding culture.

Every part of me was tingling, and I felt a shiver down my spine as I sat on the sand replaying the words over and over in my mind: *Your only work is to love yourself, value yourself, and embody this truth of self-worth and self-love so that you can be love in action. That is true service, to yourself and to those who surround you.*

I looked out toward the sea and closed my eyes, putting my hands together over my heart in gratitude, said "Thank you! I understand!" Then I got up and started walking back toward home.

I was excited to feel this renewed sense of purpose and direction, as well as a sense of trust that my life would unfold the way it was meant to unfold. I felt rejuvenated and connected with the universe once more, and I knew that as long as I stayed true to myself and remembered to recharge my batteries by being aware of my infinite connection with the universe, everything would unfold synchronistically.

What This Book Will Explore

As a result of being able to feel both the pain lodged in so many hearts all around the world along with a strong desire to bring joy back into everyone's life, I became inspired to write the book you are now reading. *What If* This *Is Heaven?* is my attempt to debunk some of the biggest myths we have been buying into—myths that have prevented us from fully living our lives simply because they have been the dominant beliefs in our surrounding culture. And just as I remembered the simple truth that set my heart free that day I sat on the beach, talking to the universe, I hope that as you read the words here, your heart will resonate with the truth you have always known deep inside and that you will feel the same freedom and joy that I did.

I believe we are born knowing the truth of who we are. But we reject this knowledge as we grow up and try to fit in and conform to society, conditioning ourselves to its norms. We learn to look outside ourselves for guidance, and in doing so, we take on other people's expectations for us. Then when we can't live up to all these external expectations, we feel inadequate and flawed.

This means that as we navigate through life, the beliefs making up the very foundation that our personal values are based on are all untrue! So no matter how many self-development workshops we take or how many self-help books we read, we still keep going outside ourselves for answers. Not only does this not serve us, it also actually holds us back! Nothing can change these destructive patterns until we break open the myths and reveal the lies that have been informing our thoughts and beliefs.

Each chapter of this book will highlight a common myth that most of us have just accepted as truth and show how these myths are pervasive and often invisible to us. I will share stories and examples from my life where I see the myths playing out, explaining how I discovered their falseness from my own experience and what I found to be true for me. Following each chapter is a section called "Living Heaven *Here and Now*," in which I'll suggest some possible truths behind the myth I just explored and outline methods for overcoming some of this conditioning so you can turn the myth around in your own life and finally live from your truth instead.

Had the last few years been a complete walk in the park, I probably wouldn't have had another book in me—at least not yet. So I thank you, all of you, for the gift of sharing your lives with me and for opening up your hearts and souls to me. Each and every one of you who has ever reached out to me has inspired me to write this book. We are all connected, and I feel what you feel. This book is my gift to you, from my heart to yours.

MYTH:
YOU GET WHAT
YOU DESERVE

"Sambo, Sambo, little black Sambo!" chanted the kids on the playground as they circled around me, taunting me because of my darker skin and frizzy hair. "Little Black Sambo," a dark-skinned southern Indian boy, was a character in a children's book we were reading in class, and enduring this merciless teasing was retribution for the privilege of studying at a private British school.

My face burned with embarrassment and shame as my eight-year-old mind filled with confusion, not knowing how to react as the circle closed in tighter on me. *Why are they doing this?* I wondered, feeling incredibly helpless. *I can't do anything about the way I look! What shall I do? Shout back? Try to hit them? Tell the teacher?*

I felt trapped, unable to move. My eyes darted around, looking for the teacher on recess duty. I finally spotted her, but she was at the other end of the playground, laughing with a group of kids who were playing cat's cradle and wanted her to join in their game. I didn't stand a chance of her noticing me—she'd never be able to hear me anyway over all the noise created by the hundreds of children on the playground skipping rope, playing catch, and so on. My tormentors had made sure they were far enough away from the teacher before starting their tirade of name-calling.

Fighting back tears, I tried to run, hoping to break through the circle closing in on me. But even as I tried to push through, the girls continued to surround me, staying close and pulling at my backpack to prevent me from getting away until we reached the stone wall of the school building on the edge of the playground.

Six Little Bullies

How I wished that the sky would open up with a clap of thunder and that one of those superheroes from the television programs I watched would come flying in and strike those playground bullies down, swooping me up to safety as I laughed at them all! But at that point, I truly would have settled for something far less dramatic—like someone, anyone, maybe even one of the other girls, suddenly standing up for me and turning against her peers. My imagination was racing with all the options I wished were happening in that moment—but alas, none of them manifested.

So there I stood, with my back against the wall and six bullies towering over me. I was invisible to everyone else in the world except those six girls, all of them much taller than I was. I briefly considered kicking them in the legs in an attempt to break free, but all I could manage to do was press myself harder and harder against the wall, trying to back away from them as far as I could, as I closed my eyes and waited for them to do their worst. Suddenly, the tallest of them, a girl named Lynette, grabbed me by the shoulder straps of my backpack and almost lifted me off the ground. I was left balancing on my tiptoes as she yanked on the straps, looked me right in the eye, and hissed, "Give us your lunch money, Sambo!"

I was sobbing by now, unable to control the tears that were streaming down my cheeks. I felt myself trembling as she loosened her grip so that I could reach in my bag for the money my dad had given me that morning to pay for juice and a snack during recess. Just as I was about to give the coins to Lynette, the school bell rang.

Lynette snatched the money out of my hand, and all of the girls turned around and started running toward the entrance of the building, where they would soon continue their day as though nothing had happened. As they ran off, my legs buckled under me and I felt myself sliding down to the ground. I just lay there for a while, in a fit of uncontrollable sobs.

Golliwog Out of Water

As an Indian child in a British school back when Hong Kong was a British colony, I was indeed a rare exception. I still remember the day earlier in that same school year when my mother took me for my admission interview with the headmistress—a stern-looking lady with a short bob hairstyle. Her demeanor conveyed that I was lucky to be given an opportunity to study in this august institution, and therefore I should be grateful for the privilege.

Once I began attending, not only did the kids taunt me on the playground with the epithet "Little Black Sambo," but they also called me a *golliwog* (or the more derogatory *wog*), after a black-skinned character with big red lips, frizzy hair, and wide eyes that was popular in children's books in my part of the world. Because I got good grades quite easily, they also called me a goody two-shoes. They would even break into my locker to steal my stuff—like my new colored pencils—just to prove they could. Through all this, I was so painfully shy and introverted that I never fought back, continuing to make myself an easy target.

At times, all the bullying would get to me so badly that I would hide in a cubicle in the girls' bathroom and cry until I had no more tears to shed. I remember many nights when I cried myself to sleep, as well. I felt as though I was backed into a corner that was so deep and so dark that there was no way to escape. Despite my good grades, I hated school with a vengeance.

The taunts embarrassed me because I felt as though being darker skinned was something to be ashamed of. I was also convinced that there must be something wrong with the way I behaved or the things I said to bring on this behavior from others.

But I couldn't figure out what I was doing or saying wrong so that I could change it and make the kids finally like me. I soon started to believe that I truly *was* a failure and wasn't as good as everyone else.

Because I was sure this was all somehow my fault, I would never talk about it to anyone, not my teachers nor even my own parents. I especially didn't want to disappoint my mother and father, who thought I was doing really well at school. At some level, I may also have sensed that reporting the bullies would only make them angrier and perhaps lash out more or get even with me for reporting them.

Another factor that worked against me was that I came from a culture rife with gender disparity, where women are considered second-class citizens. I was well aware of this disparity even from a very young age. While this didn't directly play into my experience being bullied, because the children who taunted me were all girls, it did serve to reinforce my low self-esteem in other situations in which I was mistreated.

Riyana's Betrayal

At one point that year, I became friends with another Indian girl named Riyana, who was in the year above me. She was bullied too, and we soon became very close. It felt so good to have a best friend; for the first time, I felt I could share everything that was happening to me with someone else. We stuck together, believing that we could fight off the bullies that way. We would defend each other and watch each other's backs.

We found secret hideouts within the school's vast labyrinth of hallways and grounds, places where we felt safe. We would take our snacks and lunch to these secret places, knowing no one would come and snatch them away from us. We also went to each other's homes after school, and we even slept over at each other's houses on the weekends. We were both tomboys, and we loved to ride our bikes, roller skate, and play football and cricket together.

Then one day all that changed. Apparently, Lynette and her gang had cornered Riyana during recess and threatened to beat her up. Riyana, in a moment of weakness, told them she would help them gang up on me and show them where I was if they would let her go. She offered me as a bargaining chip—as a sacrificial lamb, so to speak—to get herself out of her own predicament. Lynette and her friends had agreed to the deal.

So imagine my shock when Lynette and her gang, singing their familiar taunt of "Sambo, Sambo!" found me in one of our favorite hiding places. But my surprise was *nothing* compared with the shock and horror of seeing that Riyana was one of them! Instead of my best friend coming to my rescue and taking my side, she had led them right to me! I was so hurt by the way she turned against me that her betrayal felt much worse than the bullying. This, more than anything else, made me feel truly unworthy as a person.

Looking back now, I recognize how much being bullied scarred me emotionally and changed me at a very deep, core level. It made me want to become invisible so I could go about my business unnoticed. It made me fearful of others, and I made sure that I always flew under the radar, never joining activities like drama or student government that would have drawn attention to me. I dressed down instead of following the trendy fashions that the other kids enjoyed. I hated team sports because I knew I would be the last to be picked to join a team. I also disliked working in groups because I knew no one wanted me in theirs.

Although my mother tried relentlessly to bring me out of my shell, I remained very shy and withdrawn for much of my young life because fundamentally, I felt unlovable, flawed, ugly, repulsive, and worthless. More than once, I thought the only way out would be to take my life. *That will teach them!*, I remember thinking around the age of 13. The idea almost felt heroic, as if I would be sacrificing my life for every child who had ever been bullied. The authorities would surely sit up and take notice—especially if I left a note explaining why I had made this horrendous choice. Even the bullies themselves would be shocked, possibly to the point that they'd want to change their ways.

But in the very next moment, I would think of how commit-ting suicide would simply devastate my beloved mother, who I knew loved me unconditionally. Thinking of her in those desper-ate moments was enough to dispel any thought of taking my life. Even briefly imagining how she would mourn my death would make me cry even more, dissolving any plan before I really gave it the chance to take shape.

After all, I had already experienced my mother mourning the death of a child. When I was eight, we lost my two-year-old brother, who had Down syndrome and was born with a hole in his heart. I will never forget how his death devastated my parents and how long it took for my mother to overcome her grief. That mem-ory alone is probably the biggest reason why I am still here today.

Teenage Angst

As I grew into my teens and entered puberty, I found myself wanting to hide my changing body under loose and baggy cloth-ing so as not to draw attention to myself. I let my hair grow long because disappearing under my thick mane gave me a feeling of safety and protection. I went through school pretty much hoping no one would notice me because I believed that if no one saw me, they wouldn't be able to pick on me.

While the other kids hung out together and joined all kinds of after-school activities (like organized sports) and went to fun weekend gatherings (like school dances), I stayed away. I didn't want to go and then feel left out. I much preferred to go home after school and either spend time with my family or be by myself, listening to music or reading. Sometimes our family would go on outings with other families, and I enjoyed those, but I never, ever shared with anyone what was happening to me at school. It remained my shameful secret.

Of course, not all of my childhood was bad—in fact, much about my life was amazing and magical, especially being exposed to so many different cultures and languages in Hong Kong. I wouldn't trade the experience of having grown up there for anything now.

But the damage to my psyche had already been done. The time bomb had started ticking, waiting to explode at a much later stage of my life.

Bullying, as with any form of abuse in childhood, changes us in a very deep and fundamental way. If it starts young enough and goes on long enough, bullying can permanently affect how we view the world and how we perceive ourselves as we relate to others—even long after the teasing has ended. When this is a child's early experience, it alters their expectations for what the rest of their life is going to be like. Not surprisingly, I spent the early years of my life actually *expecting* to be rejected. My behavior in allowing this to continue merely reflected my own feelings about myself—feelings that persisted for many, many years to come.

As a result, I grew up thinking that I needed to work really hard to prove myself at every stage of my life—to prove my worth in general and to prove that I was deserving of anything positive that came my way. The experience also made me extremely sensitive to receiving negative criticism, which I would exaggerate in my own head. But possibly the biggest effect the bullying had was that whenever people did give me positive attention, I would feel undeserving and unworthy of their praise, and then I would either reject the attention or I'd be overly grateful for it. Consequently, I'd end up going out of my way to prove to them that I was indeed worthy of their positive attention—sometimes to the point of making myself a doormat.

In short, bullying stripped me of my sense of self-worth.

Learning the Truth About Love

You can imagine, then, my utter amazement during my NDE at finding that not only was I worthy of being unconditionally loved just for being me, but that I was also truly a beautiful, magnificent, and powerful creation of the universe—unique, special, and valued in every way. I didn't have to *do* anything to be worthy of this gift. I didn't have to sow any special seeds in order to reap the deep, abiding love the universe felt for me. I didn't need to prove anything, accomplish anything, or become anything. This was just the way it was, as surely as the sun sets in the evening and comes up again the next morning.

In the crystalline light of the near-death realm, I understood that none of the things I had experienced in school had anything to do with me. The kids had just been acting out their own insecurities because they, too, felt unloved and powerless. Yet they were loved by the universe just as much and just as deeply as I was. They, too, were beautiful and amazing—although like me, they didn't know it. They had projected their own sense of worthlessness onto me because they could, not because I had done anything to deserve such treatment.

Amazingly, I also saw that nothing either they or I had done required forgiveness. We had all simply acted out of ignorance because of what we'd been spoon-fed by society—a society that had also lost the knowledge of its divinity. What we experienced, warts and all, was part of the necessary journey to finding our way back to unconditional love.

Living Heaven *Here and Now*

If "You get what you deserve" is a *myth*, then what could be the *truth*?

Consider These Possible Truths

- No matter what people think or say about each other, we are all worthy of being loved unconditionally just for being who we are. We don't have to earn love—it is our birthright.

- In the other realm, each of us is recognized as a beautiful, magnificent, and powerful creation of the universe—unique, special, and valued in every way.

- No matter what we say or do (and even if it were true that no one on earth loves us), the universe has a deep, abiding love for everyone—after all, we are all connected, all part of one whole.

Tips and Exercises

- When others put you down in any way, realize their actions are direct projections of their own state of pain and confusion. Likewise, remember that opening your heart and having compassion for them in their pain (which does *not* at all mean condoning their behavior) benefits you as well as them.

- Whenever you feel others are making your life difficult, imagine what insight or skill you'd need to best deal with the situation. Then realize that it's within your grasp or the universe wouldn't be offering this situation to you. If you can see what's happening as an opportunity for growth instead of an oppressive burden, what you need to overcome the challenge will come quicker.

- Imagine you and your tormentors as actors in a play—and then visualize meeting up with them at the cast party after the show, where they are no longer in character. Picture them with completely different and very loving personalities, greeting you with genuine affection and complimenting you on your own performance. Repeat this visualization often, allowing it to help you shift your perspective a little more each time.

- Visualize revisiting an ugly incident from your past, and imagine yourself handling this

past hurt in a different way, from an older
and wiser perspective that draws upon all
you have learned in your life and now know.
Make the visualization as realistic as possible,
and be sure the outcome you envision is
empowering for *all*, not just for yourself.

- Learn techniques like tapping (Emotional
Freedom Technique), breathing exercises,
or meditation to help diffuse anxiety and
emotional reactions that keep you stuck in
the past so that you can instead live in the
present moment.

Questions to Ask Yourself

- What are my worst traumas and humiliations
from the past? What common elements or
themes do they share?

- Is it possible that others feel that *I* have
victimized *them*—even in small, unintended
ways? With this in mind, can I recognize that
some painful incidents from my past may
have been perpetrated unintentionally or that
I misconstrued what was said or done?

- What would it take for me to accept that I
am worthy of the universe's unconditional
love? What is one small thing I could do
that would bring me closer to accepting that
more fully?

*I know I am enough just as I am, without having to prove
my self-worth, when . . .*

- I can stay present and centered when others
are trying to push my buttons and provoke a
reaction (or when they are behaving in ways

that would previously have elicited a strong emotional reaction from me).

- I do not define my self-worth by external factors, such as what I look like or what I have achieved.

- I think less in terms of *what I deserve* and more in terms of *who I am*—pure love and pure consciousness.

MYTH:

LOVING YOURSELF
IS SELFISH

I was sitting on the ferry that took me from the village of Discovery Bay (where I lived until recently) across the water to Hong Kong, and I was daydreaming. I loved taking the ferry, and the 23-minute ride always felt too short. Sitting by a window if I could, I'd look out at the other ships and boats, as well as at the waves. I'd watch the seagulls dive and squawk, playing tag with each other and chasing scraps of bread or other goodies passengers threw to them. At night, I'd admire the city skyline, lit up like one of the firework displays that are so common during any of the multitude of holidays and celebrations Hong Kong has throughout the year. What an amazing sight!

On this particular day, since I was one of the first people to board, I had about ten minutes to wait before the ferry pulled out. So I took my usual window seat and gazed out onto the water as my mind started drifting, finding the currents of its own thoughts. Memories surfaced of the bullying I suffered as a child and then how I had been diagnosed with cancer and nearly died in February 2006. Finally, my mind sifted through images of what my life was like now.

I thought about how my childhood experience of being teased and ostracized had set me up to believe that I was inferior and flawed. I had lived my life believing that my ethnicity and skin color were somehow substandard and that I had to constantly prove myself to others to be accepted and liked. And being born into a culture where women were considered inferior to men certainly didn't help. So all in all, it wasn't surprising that I grew up with very low self-esteem.

Even though my parents loved me, their Hindu culture informed their thinking and shaped their lives, and they in turn passed their beliefs on to me. But when my mother and father were growing up in India, everyone else shared those same beliefs and values. Unlike them, I had to integrate these beliefs into a very different backdrop because my classmates were mostly from the U.K. and had an entirely different set of beliefs and values from those of my family.

Over the years, all of these various factors continued to shape my self-image and my identity—which was not an accurate or authentic representation of who I really was. But like most people, I rarely if ever questioned my fundamental core values and beliefs. They simply became my truth. You might say they became part of my operating system.

I know now that each thought we think is actually part of a vast network of thoughts, beliefs, and ideas that we've continued to construct over our lifetime. In other words, even what seems like a single thought—say, a thought born during a ferry ride to Hong Kong—is actually not isolated. Every thought comes as a result of all the thoughts we had before it, including the stories we tell ourselves, our beliefs, our abilities, our strengths, our weaknesses, our ideas, and so on. So even what seems like a random thought popping into our head is actually intertwined with everything we've ever experienced.

I also know now that operating out of my underlying feelings of inferiority, as well as feeling unworthy and undeserving, were the root causes of my cancer—the cancer that should have killed me. The doctors were certain I was not going to make it, and I believed them. I sensed their fear and I made it mine. I thought back to those days when I would lie in bed fearing this beast that was ravaging my body, afraid to go to sleep in case I never woke up again . . . and then I'd wake up in the morning, wishing it had all been a bad dream, only to realize that it wasn't.

I now realize that if I had known then what I know today, I would never have gotten cancer. Sitting on the ferry in my reverie, I fantasized about being able to go back in time and comfort the nine-year-old me. I started thinking about what I would tell her.

I would want her to know how loved she is and how perfect and beautiful and valued she is. I would want her to know how cruel kids can be, and that all the bullying really wasn't about her at all. I would want her to know that there's absolutely nothing wrong with her, that she is magnificent just the way she is, and that the bullies were bullying out of their own insecurities. They were weak, not strong. They were fearful, not fearless. And *that's* why they were picking on her—not because of the color of her skin or the texture of her hair or anything else about her.

My mind then drifted to where my life is now—a much more fun and joyful place filled with traveling all over the world to speak in front of large audiences at conferences with people like Wayne Dyer, Louise Hay, and Deepak Chopra. My life is a place of constant excitement, where I feel I am contributing to the lives of others. It's a place I could never have imagined being during the dark and depressing days of my childhood, when the whole world seemed like a murky, hellish existence that was just waiting to devour me.

At the same time, I have no idea how my life would have turned out had I known from the beginning how loved and val-ued and magnificent I truly am. Perhaps it took going through all that bullying and pain and fear for me to be able to bring the many positive things I now enjoy into my awareness. I do believe that everything that happens to us in this life is ultimately for our benefit and that we can see the truth of our reality only through contrasts—so perhaps pain and fear and suffering are necessary to comprehend and appreciate what love, acceptance, beauty, and joy actually feel like.

Irene

Whatever the case, I am now following my passion. I love speaking to the various audiences all over the globe and still thoroughly enjoy the traveling. Well . . . except that flying across different time zones does get physically tiring. In fact, as I sat ruminating on the ferry, I was still feeling the effects of jet lag from my last trip. Stifling a yawn, I was suddenly jolted out of my daydream by the sound of a familiar voice calling my name.

"Hey, Anita! It's so good to see you! Do you mind if I sit here?"

The voice belonged to Irene, a friend from my neighborhood. Momentarily glancing out the window, I realized we hadn't even pulled out from the pier yet. It felt as though much more time had passed. Situations like this always trigger a memory of what it was like for me coming out of the coma back in 2006. I had only been in the coma for 30 hours, but it felt like years.

"Hi, Irene!" I called out, enthusiastically returning her greeting. "Please *do* sit here. It's *great* to see you!"

Although Irene was glamorously dressed, wearing a designer top over fitted jeans, and her short dark hair was cut in a spunky style, her demeanor and facial expression told a different story. She looked tired and drained, older than her 40-something years. As she sat down next to me, she asked me how I'd been doing.

"I'm doing great!" I said. "What about you?"

"I'm okay," she replied. She immediately thought better of it and adding, "Well to be honest, I'm *not* doing that well. I'm still facing issues at work. My boss is walking all over me, and I'm working fairly long hours. My home life isn't much easier. My daughter complains that I don't spend enough time with her, and my relationship with my boyfriend is a bit precarious at the moment. It's all taking a toll on me. I'm exhausted."

Irene's life had not changed in all the years I had known her. She was always struggling with her job, her daughter, her finances, and her relationships. Many years ago, Irene and I would spend hours talking with each other about everything that was wrong with our lives. We would commiserate about how fed up we were and how tough life was, and we would compare notes on all the ways we were sacrificing ourselves and our lives for other people so that *they* could have what *they* wanted. Basically, we both believed we were victims of life's circumstances, thinking everyone else was selfish while we were selfless and giving. We never for one moment believed that we had anything to do with creating these circumstances.

And now here we were, years later—and Irene's story had not changed much. Some of the characters were different, but it was the same story line. Mind you, I was not judging her. I was aware that I could very easily still be in her shoes. Irene could be me in a parallel life, had I not experienced all I had gone through. Getting cancer, experiencing death, and returning to this life had all felt like a reboot—one that completely changed me and the way I viewed life.

"Aww, Irene, I'm so sorry to hear that you're going through such a tough time," I responded. "What's going on?"

"Where shall I start?" she asked, jumping at the invitation to offload her burden.

"Let's start somewhere fun," I suggested. "What's Natalie up to?" I asked about her daughter in an attempt to lighten the conversation, thinking that surely whatever cute little Natalie was doing couldn't be that bad.

"Don't get me started on Natalie!" Irene retorted. "She's reached an age where she's become really defiant, and she fights with me all the time. She's a little rebel who always wants her way. She's also become very sloppy with her clothes and doesn't take care of her appearance. I spend tons of money on her, and she doesn't appreciate it at all. She has no idea of the value of money and doesn't appreciate how hard I work to earn it so that she can go to a good school and have good-quality clothes, a computer, and so on." Irene loved to dress well and wear classy clothes, and I could sense how annoyed she was that her daughter wasn't as interested in all that.

"Oh Irene, she's only 13! Isn't she just being like any other kid her age? I know I may not be in a position to say this to you, because I don't have children, but to me Natalie looks like a great kid!" I responded, hoping to lighten her mood a bit.

"She may seem like a great kid, but that's just it. She still acts like a kid! When I was her age, I was a lot more mature," Irene continued before going into a rant about all the other struggles she was currently facing.

As I sat there listening to my friend complain about her daughter, her partner, her job, and her financial situation, I sensed a feeling that used to be all too familiar to me. Underneath it all, Irene felt inadequate and unloved. And like most people, she was directing the disappointment she felt in herself toward her daughter, her partner, and everyone and everything else around her. It's always much easier for us to blame others for our failures, our frustrations, and our dissatisfactions than it is to see we have something within our own selves that needs to be healed.

Self-Love

Even though Irene wore great clothes and took care of her appearance, I could see that she didn't really love herself. She was in fact really hard on herself, and she often pushed herself too far, feeling disappointed when she didn't meet her own expectations. In fact, I sensed that her drive to be fashionable and look good came more from a need to be liked, or from a lack of self-esteem, than from a true love for herself.

I was able to recognize this in her because after all, this is exactly how *I* used to be. Until my NDE, I didn't love myself either. I didn't realize that loving ourselves is actually the *most* important thing we can do, and that it's the key to living a blissful life. This all changed only when I was able to see myself from the realm of death. From that vantage point, I was able to see myself through the eyes of the divine. I could see who I really was and how powerful and special I was in the eyes of the universe. I also saw how I had arrived at a point of near extinction as I lay dying in that hospital bed.

Imagine suddenly realizing that *none* of your beliefs, values, judgments, opinions, insecurities, doubts, and fears are actually *you*, that none of those things have anything to do with who you truly are—and that in fact, they are just the layers of filters you've accumulated from all your life's experiences. And then imagine those layers being blown open so that the truth of who you really are is laid bare for you to view in all its glory.

That's exactly what happened to me. When I was on the other side, I could see that who I truly was, without all those layers and all that baggage, was far, far greater than I had ever allowed myself to imagine! I had always forsaken myself, put myself last, always felt unworthy and unlovable. But there in that realm of death, I saw myself through the eyes of God, and I realized that far from being unloved and unlovable, I was actually a beautiful child of the universe who was loved unconditionally, *simply because I exist.* I saw that I was supremely and exquisitely magnificent, perfect in every conceivable way, and created from the divine substance of the very foundation of all that is. I understood that I was truly a being of light—as is every human being and every bit of the natural world that has ever existed, since all of nature is filled with life, and all that life is interconnected.

This revelation blew my mind. I was left awestruck with my own centrality at the core of all that is, aware that I was absolutely essential to the whole—something I never before had any inkling of. I suddenly knew I was loved, and was love, and this revelation changed my entire belief system about myself and others.

Becoming Self-Aware

So as I was sitting there on the ferry in that moment, I really, really wanted Irene to know that she too was something so much more than she believed she was, and that she didn't need to be so hard on herself. I was certain that so many of her problems would dissolve if she just knew how worthy and deserving she was of all the joys life has to offer. But in order for others to love her, Irene needed to feel lovable and worthy and deserving of others' love, which would automatically happen once she finally came to love herself.

"Irene, are you aware of how beautiful and smart you are?" I blurted out while my friend was in the middle of telling me about how her partner takes her for granted and treats her like a doormat.

"What brought that on?" she asked, pleased but surprised. Her expression up to that point had been forlorn, but all of a sudden, she lit up.

"It's the truth," I insisted. "I don't think you realize how amazing you are, which is why you are feeling that others don't see you as deserving or worthy either. You are incredibly beautiful, lovable, and worthy, but I've learned that we have to know it and feel it for ourselves internally before we can see it reflected in the world around us."

"It's all very well for *you* to believe that," she refuted, "because your life is going so well! It's easy for you to love yourself and to believe that you are incredible and amazing. But my life sucks right now, so of course I'm mad at myself! How did my life end up like this? I didn't start life wanting what I have! How could I have gotten it *so wrong*?"

"Irene, you're forgetting where I've come from!" I said emphatically. "I didn't like where I was either! But I nearly died, remember? And it was only then that I realized how important it is to love myself and to never, ever forsake myself! When I'm at speaking events, I tell my audience to love themselves like their lives depend on it because loving myself is what saved my life. Our lives *do* depend on our loving ourselves. It's what brought me back from the brink of death to where I am now! We have to love ourselves *first*, and then our lives change—not the other way around! We teach others how to treat us by the example of loving ourselves first!"

"But I've always learned that it's *selfish* to love myself first," Irene countered. Her worried look was starting to come back again. "Besides, I have a daughter to think about. I have to put her first and sacrifice many of my own needs. Otherwise, how will I get her through school and give her all the opportunities she needs to not make the same mistakes I did? I have to worry about providing for her."

I knew that Irene had spent the last ten years or so of her life working really hard, often at jobs she didn't like, because she wanted to give Natalie as many opportunities as possible. She sent Natalie to one of the best schools and enrolled her in many after-school tutorials and extra classes to ensure that she was exposed to a broad range of subjects and got good grades. This obviously put a lot of pressure on both mother and daughter.

"I know I'm not a mother," I said, "but all of us have mothers, and we have all been children, so speaking for myself, I know that the best gift that my parents could have given me would have been the gift of teaching me to love myself. I believe that when parents sacrifice themselves and put all their needs last, this is what they are teaching their children. Kids learn by what their parents do, not by what they say.

"Coming from an environment of bullying, mistreatment, and despair did not set me up to love myself," I continued. "Instead, I internalized all the fear and negativity heaped upon me, and I felt in my heart that I was not only flawed, but also undeserving and unworthy of being loved, valued, and cherished. As I grew into adulthood, this core belief shaped much of who I thought I was.

"I also bought into a cultural belief that girls were inherently inferior—a burden to be avoided if possible. And like you, I was taught that it's selfish to love myself or to put myself before anyone else. As a girl, I was expected to make my life about serving others. I know that you and I are not alone in this belief. Whenever I conduct a workshop, I ask for a show of hands as to how many in the audience were taught growing up that it's selfish to love yourself—and every single time, 99 percent of the people in the audience raise their hands! I don't know why this still surprises me, because I am one of those people!

"By the way," I continued, "were you taught to 'love thy neighbor as thyself' when you were a girl?"

"Of course I remember how we were taught that," Irene retorted. "In fact, I am constantly reinforcing this to Natalie! I want her to grow up learning the importance of treating others the way you would like to be treated yourself!"

"That's great, Irene," I said. "I think empathy for others is really important. But let me ask you this: What if you don't love yourself? How well does 'love thy neighbor as thyself' work if you don't even love *yourself*?"

That was the moment the penny dropped for Irene. I could see the expression on her face completely change and her eyes widen as the implications of what I'd just said fully hit her.

"You *really* have a point there, Anita," she said excitedly. "This is what you mean when you ask, 'How can we give what we do not have?' isn't it?"

"Exactly!" I exclaimed. "It's *impossible* to truly love others until we learn to love ourselves unconditionally first. The myth that loving ourselves is selfish is the *complete opposite* of what we need to believe in order to really live our lives fully and joyfully. This is why it feels to me as though we live in an upside-down world where we are taught the opposite of what would truly help us in life. And those of us who stumble upon the truth about how important it is to love ourselves are often judged for practicing that truth, which makes many of us afraid to admit that's what we believe. That's why this truth is such a well-kept secret."

Irene seemed intently focused on what I was saying, so I kept going.

"But you must understand—unless I love myself, nothing else in my life can function at its best. The depth, meaning, and joy I experience every day—and the amount of love, kindness, and patience I have for others—is in *direct proportion* to how much love I have for myself. After all, as you just said, we cannot give others what we ourselves do not have. It's also true that the amount of love, respect, support, and compassion I *receive* from others is in direct proportion to how much I love myself, because it's impossible to receive something unless I have a place to put it.

"By *not* loving ourselves," I continued, "we are denying the part of God that expresses itself through us! And we deny it because we are conditioned to believe that loving ourselves—or even worse, *admitting* that we love ourselves—is terribly egotistical and narcissistic. But nothing could be further from the truth. Narcissism is born from its opposite—a lack of self-love and an obsession with seeking attention from others to compensate for the love we are not giving ourselves."

After I laid all this out, we both just sat there for a long minute.

Toward Self-Healing

"Hey, I just thought of something!" Irene suddenly exclaimed, breaking the silence. "I actually must love myself because I do take care of myself. I mean, I eat healthy, I like to dress well, and I always do my hair and nails and things like that! Doesn't that mean I love myself?"

"I think it's wonderful that you take the time to do these things for yourself, and I admire that about you," I responded. "But those actions aren't really the same thing as showing love to yourself," I said, remembering that I used to be fanatical about my health before I got cancer.

In fact, I'd been the poster child for eating healthy food. My diet was strictly organic, vegan food, and I would juice every day. I even grew my own wheatgrass! I was obsessive about whatever I put into my mouth. I surfed the Internet all the time, compulsively researching supplements, health foods, and the newest super-foods. I did everything possible to avoid cancer. Yet I got cancer.

When I was in the other realm, where the layers upon layers of my values and beliefs were stripped away and I was left facing the truth of who I am at my core, I learned that two primary forces—love and fear—had been driving all my behaviors. One or the other of these two forces was behind every single action I ever took, and I could clearly see that I'd in fact spent most of my life being driven by fear, not love. I understood with a sudden stunning clarity that to transform my life, whatever I said or did from that point on would need to come from a place of love instead of fear.

When I had been doing all those things to be healthy, it was the fear of getting cancer that was driving my obsessive behavior, not self-love. (Although I did not express this to Irene, I sensed that her self-care was also coming from a place of fear.) Now when I choose to eat healthy or do anything else that's good for me, I do it because I love myself and I want to live a long and healthy life. Instead of being obsessive, I'm pretty relaxed about it now because my actions are not driven by fear. I know I'm not going to get cancer if I enjoy an ice cream while watching the sunset.

To be clear, I didn't think Irene—or anyone else, for that matter—was going to get cancer just because she did things out of fear (and anyway, I hoped our conversation might have altered Irene's views on self-love). But I do think that society doesn't encourage us to be self-aware enough to understand what motivates us to do what we do. Many people actually believe that loving themselves means being in denial of their weaknesses and seeming failures and instead talking themselves up with affirmations. But that's missing the point.

Self-love is not just about constantly giving yourself praise and telling yourself how awesome you are. It's about loving the *real* you, the human you—the person who has feet of clay, who comes undone under criticism, who sometimes fails and disappoints others. It's about making a commitment to yourself that you will stick by yourself—even if no one else does!

That's what I mean when I say you must love yourself as though your life depends on it, because quite simply, I know without a doubt that it *does*!

Living Heaven *Here and Now*

If "Loving yourself is selfish" is a *myth*, then what could be the *truth*?

Consider These Possible Truths

- Because we cannot give what we do not have, loving ourselves is absolutely necessary before we can truly love anyone else. (For example, we cannot love our neighbor as ourselves if we do not first love ourselves.)

- The more we love ourselves, the more love we will have to give others because love grows exponentially (we can't use up the love we feel).

- If we are all expressions of God/Universal Energy/Creation, then *not* loving ourselves would be the same as saying that God/Universal Energy/Creation is not worth loving.

Tips and Exercises

- Each day, write down five positive traits about yourself. They can be anything positive, like how you handled a tough situation, how you care for your family, a talent or ability you possess, or even a physical trait you admire. Keep a journal of these daily lists, so that later on, you can look back at what you wrote. We tend to habitually criticize ourselves, so the purpose of this exercise is to retrain our mind to notice our positive qualities instead of our negative ones.

- If you have a partner, spouse, friend, or family member whom you trust, make a commitment with this person to spend just five minutes each day identifying the positive qualities each of you sees in the other. This will heal or strengthen any relationship, and it will also elevate your own self-esteem.

- When you wake up each morning, look straight into your eyes in the mirror and say out loud, "I love you. I will never let you down, forsake you, or treat you like a doormat. I will always be your best friend!" Modify those words to reflect whatever feels right to you. (Feel free to repeat this exercise whenever you feel the need throughout the day.)

Questions to Ask Yourself

- How can I love myself *more*?

- What would I be doing right now if I *did* love myself?

- How can I support myself more through whatever challenge I'm facing?

- How can I model for my children or other young people in my life how important it is for all of us to love ourselves?

I know that I'm being loving toward myself when . . .

- I allow myself to make choices that feel like fun and that bring me joy and pleasure, instead of constantly worrying about what others are going to think.

- I stop feeling guilty when my life is going well or when I am living a life of joy.

- The voice of my self-critic is no longer the loudest voice in my head.

- I stop deflecting compliments others give me and instead respond with genuine gratitude.

- What I do for others I do freely and joyfully instead of out of a sense of obligation or guilt or because I feel manipulated.

- I recognize that I have the right to be happy, even if the people around me are not in a good place or are not themselves happy.

MYTH:
REAL LOVE MEANS
ANYTHING GOES

On a chilly morning in Hong Kong, I sat down in front of my computer, adjusted my headset microphone, and prepared to receive a call from a radio show host in Southern California who was about to interview me for her live show. It was 6 A.M. for me, while for the listeners in California it was 3 P.M. the previous day. Technology amazes me—I still find it incredible that I can give a radio interview from my own home with a host based half-way around the world, while we see and hear each other live on our computer screens.

Although sharing my story via the Internet and other media outlets had by this time become a way of life for me, I was still excited about the interview that morning and had been awake for the past hour. As I lay in bed in the dark before getting up, thoughts danced around in my mind about how radically my life had changed since my near-death experience. Even now, my eyes still well up with tears whenever I think back to that day in February 2006—a day that should have been my last on earth.

I was overcome with emotion remembering the feeling of being in the other realm and becoming aware that I still had much to come back for. In that NDE state, I had seen my life unfolding in the future and was aware that I was somehow going to affect thousands—even hundreds of thousands—of people all over the world, even though I didn't know then why or how this would occur. I also knew that I wouldn't have to do anything to make it all happen. Everything would just unfold in its own way and at its own pace. Since then, it's been astonishing to watch it all transpire, seeing all the bits and pieces of the tapestry come together in the most remarkable way, far beyond anything I could ever have imagined.

While I lay there in the dark, I could hear my husband, Danny, breathing beside me as he continued to slumber. I sometimes envy his ability to stay above the hubbub, even though all the attention has certainly had an impact on him as well. After a few minutes, I quietly got out of bed, put on a terry-cloth robe, and went into the kitchen to make a cup of Darjeeling tea. I filled the kettle from the tap and put it on the stove, and in a few minutes, the kettle's whistle began to sing. I poured the water over the fragrant tea bag and let it steep.

Sitting down at my desk—which had become the place where I kept in touch with the world—I checked e-mails as I waited for the interview to start. Riana, the radio show host, called right on time. After we made our introductions, she told me she had been amazed to read about my story and wanted our interview to focus on the lessons I'd learned from the NDE and how the experience had affected my current life.

"Sure," I told her. "We can focus on anything you like." I could tell by the lightness in her voice that this was going to be a great interview. Not only was she professional, but she also came across as very genuine and loving. I knew I was going to enjoy talking to her and that she would draw out the best in me.

What Unconditional Love Really Means

Riana opened the show and introduced me to the audience, and then she asked one of my favorite questions: "You mentioned in your book that one of the biggest things you understood from your experience in the other realm was that we are all loved unconditionally. You say that realizing this truth is what healed your body from cancer. Can you expand a little bit more on that? What do you mean when you say that we are loved unconditionally?"

"Yes, absolutely," I answered, casting my mind and senses back to the expanded state of awareness I'd experienced in the other realm. Whenever I recall that state, it's as though I'm actually reliving it; it's not just like a memory. Once again, I feel all my senses become immersed in that state of oneness, completely bathed in pure, absolute, unconditional love and acceptance.

"Every time I speak about that incredible state, I feel very emotional," I told Riana. "Just thinking about it now gives me goose bumps. It was indescribable, like nothing I had ever experienced before. But let's see if I can put words to it. Being in that state made me realize that I didn't have to *do* anything to deserve being loved. I realized that I'm loved unconditionally just because I exist! In fact, even the word *unconditional* is superfluous, because love, by its true definition, is unconditional. *Conditional love* is an oxymoron—a contradiction in terms. As soon as we put conditions on love, it becomes something else entirely."

I looked directly at Riana's image on my computer screen as I spoke, and I could see she was looking back at me intently. I leaned closer to the monitor as I continued.

"When we are in that state of consciousness beyond our body, everything becomes known," I explained. "We understand. The clarity is astounding, incomparable to anything we can imagine here in the physical world. It's like waking up from a deep sleep after a complex and terrifying nightmare—and then being relieved that the whole thing was just a dream. That's how it felt when I woke up in the other realm and realized that I was not my sick body."

"That sounds really powerful!" Riana said, chiming in. "In fact, it *is* powerful because realizing that you are loved unconditionally healed you of your cancer.

"The questions from our listeners are pouring in like crazy! Here's one from someone who wants you to explain a bit more about unconditional love and how it's different from the love we feel for our loved ones, our pets, and our family."

"It would almost be like comparing the soft, cool glow from a firefly to the blazing heat and light from the sun," I answered. "When the sun is shining, we are bathed in glorious warmth and light that completely wraps us up in its brilliance. It's unconditional. The sun doesn't choose to whom it's going to give warmth and light and to whom it's not. The sun *just is*. Everyone gets bathed in its splendor, warmth, and brilliance when we are in it. And the sun never stops shining. We may not be able to see it all the time due to Earth's rotation, yet the sun itself never stops giving its light for any reason. When we are turned away from the sun, someone on the other side of Earth is turned toward it.

"The firefly's small glow, on the other hand, has much less power; and it's much more discriminating, more selective, and more conditional. You have to be in a direct line of sight with the firefly to see its light, and even then, it's really easy to miss or lose sight of. It's beautiful in its own way, but rather paltry compared with the sun. You have to keep focused on the firefly, working at following it as it flits here and there, if you want to keep seeing its light. That's what earthly love feels like in comparison with the full-out, unconditional love of the other realm.

"One of the insights I gained from my NDE is that unconditional love is a state of being, not an emotion. That means it has no opposite. Human love is an emotion, and as with all other emotions, it's part of duality. An opposite emotion, such as fear or hate, balances it out. But unconditional love just *is*. It's not one side of the coin—it's the *whole* coin!"

"Beautifully said!" Riana responded, smiling. "I just can't imagine how awesome it must be to experience that kind of love and acceptance, no matter what we may have done in the past. It must really have been overwhelming."

"It *was* overwhelming," I agreed, "and even now I can't imagine that state without tears welling up and spilling over. There's really nothing here in the physical realm to compare it with."

"That's just amazing!" Riana said. "I think this unconditional love you speak of can give us all something to look forward to. It sounds positively glorious!"

Self-Love's Role

"Okay, here's a really interesting question that I'm curious about myself," she said, reading an e-mail a listener had just sent. "A woman asks how she can love someone unconditionally who abuses her and doesn't treat her well. She says her boyfriend takes her for granted, even though she tries to love him unconditionally by completely accepting everything he does and giving him more and more love. But their relationship never gets any better. She says this 'unconditional love' thing is not working for her."

Hearing this, I immediately grinned.

"I love that question," I said, "because thinking that loving others unconditionally means allowing them to treat you however they please is one of the most misunderstood concepts I come across in the letters that people write to me! True unconditional love starts with the self. This is why I keep harping on the importance of self-love. When you love yourself, you will never allow anyone to use you or abuse you!

"If our loved one's values go against our own, we need to love ourselves enough to be able to leave the relationship without resentment or animosity, instead of staying just for the sake of holding on to the relationship, which can be soul destroying.

"When you are willing to walk away from a relationship that is damaging to your soul, usually one of two outcomes happens. One possibility is that when your partner realizes you're willing to walk away because you will not tolerate being treated this way, they will be forced to change their behavior if they value the relationship. Alternatively, if they don't change and you do walk away, you are opening yourself up for someone else to come into your life who can love and value you for who you are, not for who they want you to be!

"I want to add that true, authentic, unconditional love means wanting for others what they want for themselves, regardless of whether it goes against what we want for ourselves in the relationship. So we need to set our partners free to be who they are, not expect them to contort themselves to fit our ideas of who we want them to be. The real test is to ask ourselves, *Does this relationship support freedom, or does it feel like bondage?* We need to be honest with ourselves when we answer. Relationships based on unconditional love are freeing. Those couples are together because they choose to be together, not because they feel trapped."

"That's spot on!" Riana exclaimed. "But can you tell me what relationships look like when we are truly able to express love unconditionally? You and Danny seem to have this kind of relationship, so I'm curious to know how it works and why."

"Beautiful question," I began. "First of all, you're right. Danny and I *do* have a relationship based on unconditional love. That doesn't mean that everything is *always* totally peachy or without challenge, but it does mean that we allow each other to be who we truly are.

"For example, we are both very different in our needs, our wants, and our approaches to life. Danny loves technology and gadgets. He also enjoys an occasional cigar. He prefers being indoors in front of his computer to going out. He doesn't like sweets, but he likes eating either a pepperoni pizza or a Whopper double cheeseburger while watching *Battlestar Galactica* or *NCIS* on television. I, on the other hand, crave chocolate and desserts, have a handbag and shoe fetish, can't find enough different kinds of perfumes or elaborately embroidered shawls, prefer vegetarian food when there's a choice, enjoy listening to soft and soothing music, love being outdoors in nature (particularly sitting by the ocean listening to the waves), and can actually cry over a beautiful sunset. Obviously, such differences could result in more than a few disagreements, but we have very few of those, even though we spend a lot of time together and are rarely apart. Neither of us tries to change the other. We simply give each other the respect we deserve, and we celebrate our differences. We also learn a lot from each other—we've both changed and grown as a result of what we have learned from our relationship.

"In a mature relationship, there's pure acceptance *for* both parties *by* both parties," I added. "And paradoxically, when there's acceptance, there's usually no reason to leave the relationship even if the parties don't share the same values.

"Danny and I agreed on a few nonnegotiable core values right from the beginning. No matter how angry we felt, we agreed never to give each other the silent treatment. In other words, communication channels had to always stay open. We also agreed never to go to bed angry at each other, which we've stuck to even after 20 years of marriage—not out of obligation, but out of love. Neither of us would ever want it any other way.

"More recently," I added, "after my experience on the other side, Danny and I hug each other every single morning after we wake up, and we say 'I love you' to each other before we start our day.

"Two very different people can love each other and coexist very happily if they truly accept each other and agree not to judge each other. Problems arise only when one or both imposes their own values and preferences on the other, judging the other negatively. In many relationships, one partner is fearful of relinquishing control, fearing that if they let go of the control they seem to have over the relationship, they'll lose their partner. So they hold on to them tightly through manipulation and control. That's not a loving relationship at all, and not surprisingly, the person who wants control ends up pushing their partner away. In an unconditionally loving relationship, on the other hand, two people are together because they *want* to be, not because they feel they *have* to be. Currently, many couples stay together because of a marital contract, whether they love each other or not. One day, I hope we will all be mature enough to be in relationships only out of choice, not because of fear, obligation, or manipulation."

"That's really useful information," Riana commented. "That's the way relationships of the future need to be heading! With divorce rates as high as they are now, I think the way we look at marriage and relationships needs to be seriously challenged!

"There is so much more I want to talk to you about on this subject, but first we need to take a break and hear from our sponsors. After we come back, I want to ask you about what your relationship was like before your near-death experience and how much it changed afterward. Stay tuned, everybody. We'll be back in a jiffy with more questions for Anita Moorjani . . ."

As I listened to the bumper music that Riana cued to transition from the show to the commercials, my thoughts drifted to what my mindset had been like before the NDE and how much it had changed since that time. I lived in so much needless fear back then. I was afraid of *everything*—including future events that were relatively unlikely to happen. My imagination had always conjured up the worst possible scenario in any situation, including a menagerie of gruesome creeps just waiting to spring out at me.

I still have certain anxieties and feelings of doom from time to time, but nothing like I did before my NDE. And now I know how to deal with them. I don't judge the fears or anxiety, nor do I try to push them away or criticize myself for feeling them—I just accept the feelings, and they eventually pass.

The sound of running water suddenly caught my attention, and I realized Danny was in the kitchen, making himself a cup of coffee. He was aware I was being interviewed live, and after he'd gotten out of bed, he'd snuck past me to the kitchen without making a sound until then. He's good at that.

"Good morning, darling!" I called out to him.

"Ah, you're on a commercial break!" Danny called back. "Do you want some more tea?"

"Yes, please!" I responded.

In fact, it's because of Danny that I am able to have access to the kind of technology that allows me to do interviews like this from my own living room. He always buys the best equipment, and he sets up everything the night before, adjusting the levels on his mixer so that I'll be ready to go at the appointed time. Interviewers often remark on the quality of the sound from my equipment, and I always tell them that my husband is a true techie geek!

The commercial break was soon over, and the bumper music faded back in and then out again, just as Danny brought me another cup of tea.

"Welcome back, everybody," Riana said warmly. "We are talking today with Anita Moorjani, author of *Dying to Be Me*. Welcome back, Anita. Okay, let's talk about your relationship before your near-death experience. What was it like before you learned that you were loved unconditionally and that you were worthy and deserving of receiving this unconditional love?"

Loving on a New Level

"To be honest, Danny has always been very loving toward me," I answered, "but before I met him, I *had* been in relationships where I was badly mistreated. Even though I wasn't physically abused, I was certainly abused mentally and emotionally. I used to put up with a lot because I didn't want to lose the relationship. I used to believe that it was better to be in a relationship, even a bad one, than it was to be single. And I would take responsibility for everything that was wrong, taking it upon myself to make it right."

"I'll bet there are a lot of people out there, especially women, who will relate to that!" Riana responded with enthusiasm. "Give us some examples!

"Well, I once caught the man I was dating—a man who had already asked me to marry him, by the way— having a good kiss and cuddle with one of my girlfriends! And I still accepted him back after that, because the idea of marriage was so important to me! Can you imagine what a disaster that would have been? And in another relationship, the man I was dating made it clear that I was going to be a stay-at-home wife after the wedding. He expected me to cook for him, even while we were dating, and he wanted me to learn from his mother how to make all his favorite dishes. I put up with that for quite a while too, even though it was not at all what I wanted to do! I kept wondering whether there was something wrong with me for not wanting to be a stay-at-home wife!"

"So how did you meet Danny?" Riana asked.

"I met Danny while I was still dating one of these men who were not good for me," I told her. "I was out with a girlfriend one evening, and he just happened to be in the same place. When our eyes met, it was like recognition. He was different from anyone else I had met, and at first I didn't trust myself to follow through with my feelings. I'd had so many bad experiences that when Danny later called me to ask me to meet him, I didn't go because I was dating someone else—even though that someone else wasn't treating me well.

"But Danny continued to pursue me, telling me that he 'recognized' me, as though he knew me from another lifetime, and he asked me if I had felt that, as well. I *had*, but I still didn't have the courage to leave the relationship I was in.

"Fortunately, Danny was very patient, and I finally realized that he truly was the one for me! Being with him was like coming home. In many ways, he saved me—from myself *and* from the type of person I would have ended up marrying."

"Aww, God bless him! He sounds lovely!" said Riana. "But has your relationship changed since your near-death experience?"

"Yes, absolutely" I responded. "Before, I used to feel that I had to keep doing things all the time to prove to Danny that I was worthy or deserving of his love. Even if *he* never made me feel that way, *I* felt it. The community I was raised in labeled me as a very compromised woman! I had run away from an arranged marriage—an enormous taboo in my culture—and I was independent. So in their eyes, I was undomesticated, opinionated, and had a mind of my own—in other words, flawed beyond redemption. And I believed that about myself, too! So in my mind, I would think, *How could anyone possibly love someone like me?* It never occurred to me that maybe Danny loved me for who I was and that I didn't have to work at it! I mean, that's just too easy, right? So I would contort myself in all sorts of ways trying to match this or that image of the perfect wife—an image I had created in my own head—just to prove to him that I was worthy of his love.

"Only after my NDE did I realize that I was already deserving and worthy of love, and that I didn't have to work for it! It was after that realization that things began to shift even more. We already had a good relationship, but our relationship went from good to great.

"I realized that not only had I spent my entire life not loving *myself* unconditionally, but by failing to do so, I was sending myself the message that I'm not worthy of being loved, so I also wasn't allowing *others* to love me unconditionally!

"This realization alone transformed my relationship with Danny because I became free to be myself instead of who I thought Danny wanted me to be. And as soon as I started doing that, our relationship became really light and fun! And because I was able to completely accept *myself* without feeling the need to change, I was also able to accept Danny completely as well, without needing *him* to change. And then I found that the more I accepted myself, the less I judged myself—and as a result, the less judgmental I was of Danny.

"We started to have this very easy exchange of energy that flowed back and forth in a most natural way. If you were to look at it from the outside, probably the biggest difference you would see between how we used to be and how we are now is that we laugh a lot. And I really mean a lot! We laugh with each other, and we are very quick to laugh at ourselves and at what others would label as our shortcomings, but instead of using that word, we call it our *humanness*.

"The other thing you would notice looking at us from the outside is that we never criticize each other. Never. We also deliberately and consciously tell each other what we appreciate about the other, and we do this constantly."

"You guys sure are smart about your relationship!" Riana said. "You're very wise in your way of dealing with life."

"I don't actually believe that Danny and I are smarter or more loving than every other couple," I responded. "Yet looking around, I see so many people struggling to keep their relationships together—even those who are extremely generous with offering their love to others. Personally, I think the lack of self-love, or the feeling of being undeserving of being loved, is at the root of this issue. When we feel undeserving, we become incapable of receiving love, and then we end up giving and giving of ourselves and become drained. We then start to expect those around us, whom we have been giving to all this time, to repay us and help build us back up. And if that love and attention is not forthcoming, then we begin to resent those people for not being there for us when we need them. We have always been there for them, we think, so why aren't they there for us as well? This is how dysfunctional relationships are formed."

"That's an insightful point!" Riana replied. "I've truly enjoyed this hour with you, Anita, but sadly, we're almost out of time. But before we sign off, I want to touch on something else you haven't yet mentioned. What are your thoughts about service—that is, giving back? Where does that come in?"

Service As Unconditional Love

"Service will come naturally, as part of who we are, when we allow ourselves to truly express our authenticity from the center of our being," I responded. "At one time, I used to give service because I felt I 'should' and because it was the 'right' thing to do. That kind of service comes from the head, not from the heart. It comes from a feeling of obligation or a sense of duty, and it can drain our energy if we keep bowing to the pressure of continuing to serve in this way. We think we're doing good, but it doesn't occur to us that to perform a service out of obligation is dishonest both to the receiver and to the giver. If it doesn't come from a place of love, the receiver can often sense that and then feel indebted to the giver for the service. It becomes an unhealthy cycle.

"True service comes from the heart," I continued, "and it comes naturally to us when we allow ourselves to just be who we really are, so there's no feeling of obligation. That's when we start to *be* of service, instead of *performing* a service. At that point, service stops being a heavy burden. Instead, it feels light and fun, and it then becomes a joy that uplifts us as well as the people who benefit. Currently, I don't even think about giving service, but my sense is that I am being of service naturally, without really think-ing about it—just by being myself.

"In fact, this true service is a natural consequence of the unconditional love we were just talking about. When we tap into that feeling of being unconditionally loved, we're then better able to begin to unconditionally love ourselves and others, and we want to share that expansive, loving feeling as much as we can, as often as we can."

"Fabulous, Anita!" Riana said as the clock ticked down the hour. "What an amazing show. Thank you so much for agreeing to be interviewed today! I am certain a lot of people have ben-efited greatly from hearing what you had to share. Do you have any final words before we close?"

"Only that I would love for everyone to lighten up and laugh more!" I added. "I know I'm being preachy now, but I feel com-pelled to say this. We tend to take spirituality too seriously, and it can take a lot of the fun out of life. The most spiritual act possible is to be yourself, to love yourself, and to love your life. The best way to do that is to have fun and laugh! Don't worry about trying to be more spiritual. You already are as spiritual as you can pos-sibly be! You are perfect just the way you are right now. Celebrate that fact!"

After Riana and I thanked each other, and I told her that being on her show had been great fun for me, she said good-bye and her voice faded in the bumper music—this time a light jazz instru-mental. Hearing the beeps signaling the top of the hour, I clicked the "end call" button on my computer screen.

As I took off my headset, feeling totally buzzed, wide awake, and ready to take on the rest of my day, I thought again of how simple the concept of unconditional love is—and how compli-cated we seem to make it. On the physical plane, we see love as an emotion, something we have for some people and not others. But the truth is that unconditional love is a state of being, and it's our birthright. Once we begin to tap into that, we realize it has the power to transform all of our relationships simultaneously—including our relationship with ourselves—for the better.

Living Heaven *Here and Now*

If "Loving someone unconditionally means allowing them to treat you as they please" is a *myth*, then what could be the *truth*?

Consider These Possible Truths

- You can't love another unconditionally until you love yourself unconditionally, and when you truly do achieve that, you will never allow anyone to use you or abuse you.

- A relationship that does not involve pure acceptance *for* both people *by* both people cannot benefit either person.

- Authentic unconditional love means wanting for another what that person wants for themselves and allowing that person to be who they truly are—even if it requires setting them free—instead of expecting them to change to fit our ideas of who we want them to be.

- Relationships based on unconditional love are freeing because those couples choose to be together rather than stay together because they feel trapped by fear, obligation, or manipulation.

Tips and Exercises

- Notice that the more you completely accept and love *yourself* without judgment, the more you can love and accept your partner without needing *them* to change.

- Resist the urge to give in order to receive. Understand that true giving does not involve expectation and is completely selfless.

- When others treat you badly or think poorly of you for any reason, realize that their thoughts and actions say a lot more about *them* than they do about *you*. No matter what another person claims or how strongly they insist, you are *not* responsible for that person's feelings or behavior.

Questions to Ask Yourself

- Is this relationship supportive for both of us, or does it feel like bondage?

- Do I feel drained in this relationship, always giving more than I receive? If so, what compels me to perpetuate the imbalance by either overgiving or by staying?

- Am I often disappointed and even resentful because I feel I deserve love, acceptance, or support in direct return for what I've given others instead of because it's simply my birthright? What would it take for me to feel deserving of receiving love and support without having to give a certain amount first?

- Is my partner always calling the shots, essentially taking control and manipulating me? Do I ever mistakenly equate such manipulation with true love? Do I feel worthy of a relationship in which each of us has equal control and mutual respect?

- Do I expect my partner or other loved ones to fit into a mold I've designed instead of accepting who they truly are? How might

such expectations limit the relationship
and also hold me back from my own
spiritual growth?

I know I am experiencing true unconditional love when . . .

- I am truly happy for others when they
  discover new things about themselves and
  grow spiritually; I don't feel threatened
  by that or worry about how the situation
  affects me.

- My relationship with my partner allows each
  of us the freedom to be who we truly are, and
  we fully support each other in doing what
  makes us truly happy.

- I accept that sometimes I will give more and
  sometimes I will receive more, but overall
  my relationship reflects a healthy balance
  between giving and receiving.

MYTH:
I'M NOT OKAY,
YOU'RE NOT OKAY

O ne day when I was doing a few errands in the central business district of Hong Kong, I happened to run into a former colleague who I used to spend a lot of time with. Our lives had since grown in different directions, and I hadn't seen Victoria for quite a while. As we chatted amicably and caught up on each other's news, I was delighted we had crossed paths again.

"Where are you going?" I asked, hoping we were headed in the same direction so we could continue our discussion.

"I'm going to see Jen Tai," she responded. "Why don't you come along?"

Jen Tai is Victoria's Chinese medicine practitioner, who Victoria has been seeing for whatever happens to be ailing her at the moment (and often for nothing in particular) for years. I'd gone to see her in the past as well, although I hadn't been in a long time.

"Uh . . . no thanks," I told her. "I'm feeling great these days." As I spoke, I couldn't help but beam. I really had been feeling great—even better than I had felt before I got sick. Actually, I'd never felt more physically healthy.

"You know, all this flying you do is not good for your body," Victoria said with concern. "And all the public speaking must be so draining! Are you doing anything to counter the effects? It might be wise for you to see Jen Tai again for some additional support." I knew Victoria meant well. And I knew Jen Tai was good at what she did. But I really didn't think seeing a practitioner—of any kind—was necessary for me at the moment.

"I'm already taking some Chinese herbs that are giving me loads of energy," I countered, "so I'm good." I thanked Victoria for her concern, gave her a warm hug, and promised to stay in touch before we went our separate ways.

I now knew better than to go down the road of seeing a healer with Victoria. Like my friend, I spent most of my life believing there was something fundamentally wrong with me that needed fixing. I believed that my physical and emotional health needed constant work, as well as intervention from various experts, in order to improve. It never occurred to me that believing I needed to be fixed or "improved upon" would, in fact, have the *opposite* effect—that it would actually cause all sorts of problems, including inducing feelings of fear, insecurity, and vulnerability. In fact, I'm certain all these feelings contributed to my getting cancer. Only after nearly dying and then returning to this plane did I learn that we are actually already born with *all* the resources we will ever need. Coming back from the brink of death made me feel invincible for quite a long time.

However, a subsequent experience with Victoria made me realize how easy it is for this feeling of invincibility to erode and to fall back into my old pattern of thinking that I need fixing. For many of us, these beliefs are particularly corrosive if they're also held by our peer group or our surrounding culture—which is exactly what happened to me.

It all started a few years ago, when I used to visit Victoria at her home, not long after I'd healed from cancer. Whenever I'd enter Victoria's place, I'd always smell something medicinal wafting out of her kitchen, where she would have an herbal concoction brewing. Jen Tai kept Victoria supplied in tonics, Chinese herbs, healing teas, and so on. I remember being fascinated with these preparations and wanting to go with Victoria to see Jen Tai myself, more out of curiosity than anything else.

Although I felt completely healed from cancer and quite healthy, I had been going through a stressful time because Danny and I had just moved into a new house and we were making some major changes with work. This was before I had even started writing my first book, when I had no inkling of how my life was going to turn out. One day, I had bumped into Victoria at the grocery store in our neighborhood and I must have looked particularly tired. She asked me how I was doing.

"I'm doing great," I responded. "I'm just feeling a little bit tired from my recent move, and then on top of that, we've just taken on a huge new project at work."

"You *do* look tired," Victoria had said. "You, of all people, should know that stress is not good for your body. Are you doing anything to counter the effects? I mean, are you taking any remedies or seeing a healer or anything like that?"

"No, I just try to get plenty of rest," I answered. "All I need is a bit of sleep, and I should be fine."

"You really have to take better care of yourself," she said emphatically. "Otherwise your cancer may come back! Someone who has been as sick as you have really needs to take better care of themselves!"

"Well, I'm inclined to believe that someone who's healed from cancer as rapidly as I did has some idea how resilient the body can be!" I responded with a mischievous smile.

"Don't be so overconfident!" Victoria retorted. "You never know. Next time things might not work out so well for you."

That was typical of Victoria. Blunt and brutally honest with her opinions and feelings. I didn't recognize it at that time, but looking back on it now, I can see that she was just projecting her own fears onto me.

"It seems to me that with this new work project, you'll probably get even *less* sleep," she continued. "You're draining yourself, and I think you need to do something that replenishes your energy. I see a healer regularly because my work is really stressful, and she works magic! I wouldn't be able to survive without her!"

Something didn't quite feel right within me when Victoria said that. I couldn't put my finger on it at the time, but I later realized that although Victoria believed she was taking care of her well-being by seeing Jen Tai on a regular basis to relieve the stress she felt from work, it seemed to me she was trying to fix the problem from the wrong end.

If I really cared about myself, I wouldn't regularly take on work that was so stressful I would need help recuperating from it—not as a way of life, anyway. Sure, I inevitably push my limits every now and again; and when that happens, I reach out for support, whether I visit a healer such as Jen Tai or perhaps even go for a massage or spa treatment to help my body relax. But I don't make that into a lifestyle. I tend to check in with my emotions, and I am careful to take on work that uplifts me—work that reflects who I am and that I enjoy so much that it doesn't feel like work—so that I don't need to relieve stress on an ongoing basis.

"Jen Tai uses purely natural methods including herbs and other nature-based remedies to increase vitality," Victoria continued, still trying hard to convince me. "Why don't I take you along the next time I go see her?"

"Hmmm . . . I don't know," I replied. "I just want to focus on getting settled into my new home right now, and Jen Tai's clinic is a bit far. I don't really want to add to my already overloaded schedule."

Doubt Creeps In

"Oh, I think it will be *totally* worth your time. After all, you need to take care of yourself first!" Victoria countered, intentionally hurling my own philosophy back at me to make her point. "And Jen Tai works magic. Do you know how many people go to see her? She has queues of people waiting outside her clinic! You remember Deirdre from the Women in Business Club all those years ago? She goes to see Jen Tai all the time! She was having some health issues, and Jen Tai helped her through it. Deirdre says Jen Tai saved her life, and now Deirdre goes to see her regularly, without fail! She's been doing it for years! Anita, after all you've been through, you really owe it to yourself. You want to do everything you can to stay healthy, don't you?"

Victoria might have a point there, I thought. I knew Jen Tai was indeed skilled, and I certainly was interested in staying healthy. *It couldn't hurt to go once and just see what Jen Tai had to say. Maybe she could suggest a tonic that would boost my flagging energy a bit. That surely would be a good thing, right?*

"Well, okay," I said brightly. "I guess you're right—I know Jen Tai has a lot of expertise, and it would be fun to go with you, at least once."

But still, deep down, something just didn't feel right. My words were ringing a bit hollow. I hadn't been worried about the temporary stress I had been feeling. I was sure that once I was done with the move, I'd be fine. I was really happy with the way my life was going. I had learned from nearly dying not to take on anything that didn't feel fun or right for me—and I hadn't gone back on that commitment. What had been stressing me out recently was that I hadn't had time for my regular walks in nature or for day trips to the beach. So surely I'd be fine once I was settled in my new home—especially because my new home was closer to the ocean! I was so excited about that!

"It won't be just once. That's not how it works," Victoria said a bit sternly. "You have to make a commitment. That's the only way to support your body long term. After all, you're not getting any younger, and things will only get worse if you don't start doing something about it now!"

"I don't think I can commit to an ongoing regimen at this stage," I said, feeling a twinge of fear at Victoria's retort. "I've got so much going on!"

"You need to put your health before your work! You of all people should know this!"

Again, although I did not recognize it at that time, looking back, I can see that Victoria was projecting *her* fears onto *me*. This was how *she* would need to support herself if she were in my situation. But for me, the notion of introducing a fixed regimen like this into my life brought me nothing but more stress. Even so,

Victoria's stern words had their intended effect. The idea that my cancer might come back if I did *not* do everything I could to support my health had heightened my anxiety, making it impossible for me to see the situation clearly. I could slowly feel the wind being taken out of my sails as the dialogue progressed. I was getting sucked in.

"Actually, I've been thinking about you quite a bit recently," Victoria said next. "I've been wondering how you have been holding up, integrating back into regular life. I mean, living in a fast-paced city like Hong Kong can be so stressful—and you had *stage four* cancer," she said.

"Well, I actually really love my work, but I also spend a lot of time doing other fun things because it's so important for me to enjoy my life!" I responded. "Occasionally work gets stressful or overwhelming, but I usually handle it pretty well."

"Be careful you don't get drained and go right back into the cycle of trying to be there for everyone all over again," Victoria warned. "I hate to keep saying this, but after what you've been through, you of all people need to be careful about your health."

Getting Sucked In

My head kept swirling with the idea that maybe Victoria was right. Perhaps I looked more tired and drained than I thought. Maybe there was something deeper happening in my body, maybe because having had cancer made me more vulnerable. Victoria seemed so genuinely concerned for my well-being, which is why I did not realize in that moment that these were *her* fears and that I was starting to take on her anxieties as though they were my own.

My confidence in my own ability to know what was right for me started to recede, and now I could hear a whisper in my mind: *What if she's right? I do expend a lot of energy, working, meeting people all the time, giving of myself when asked, and being there for people who need me. I love what I'm doing, but it would be awful if I got so drained that I weakened my immune system! I must be careful or my cancer may come back! I would certainly never want to go through that again! Maybe I need to see this healer. If I really care about my health, I should do whatever I can to preserve it. At least Jen Tai is a naturopathic healer—that's got to be a good thing.*

A subtle fear had slowly crept into my psyche and was now lodging itself there. I began sensing the loss of that empowered feeling, that *knowing* what feels right and true for me, and of my body's innate ability to communicate that without constant intervention from external sources. I suddenly felt drained and stressed. Thanks to my increasing anxiety, I had forgotten that all I ever have to do is listen to my own body, just as I had learned from almost dying and just as I had been doing for the last few years since being healed of my cancer.

All I needed to do was to continue checking in with myself about what I needed, without buying into someone else telling me what that had to be. After all, this inner knowing, my internal compass, had been what healed me from end-stage cancer. But in that conversation with Victoria, all I could think was, *Maybe she's right. Maybe I should listen to her.*

Herbal Medicine

During the course of the afternoon, as I wandered through the teeming streets of downtown Hong Kong, busying myself with my many errands, that undercurrent of fear stayed with me. I tried to shake it off by focusing my attention elsewhere. I perused the street markets, stopping at the stalls to feast my soul on the assortment of colorful candies, toys, spices, meats, handbags, and blouses—I was in the midst of a veritable kaleidoscope not only of colors but also of sounds, textures, and scents.

But I was unable to completely lose myself in the experience. In the back of my head, that whispering fear nagged at me, and I found my attention continuing to return to what Victoria had said—despite my attempts to deflect it.

The following week when the feeling of heaviness still had not dissipated, I pulled out my phone and called Victoria. The fear seemed to be following me wherever I went, whatever I did, even when I was trying to have fun. I told Victoria that the next time she was planning to see Jen Tai, I would like to go. Victoria said she happened to be going the following day, so we made plans to meet.

The next morning, we greeted each other at the ferry pier before boarding the boat to Hong Kong Island. After we got off the ferry, we climbed the stairs to the overpass crossing the main six-lane highway that ran along the waterfront. From that point, I could look over the entire harbor, all the way back to Lan Tau Island where I lived. Ferries skidded across the bay like water bugs traversing a pond.

We came down the overpass on the other side and ducked down a side street, where the familiar smell of curried fish on skewers wafted through the air. As we turned the corner, I almost ran into the fish vendor, whose cart featured a big vat of boiling curry, bubbling with fish balls that he would dip out and serve on skewers to passing customers. I was tempted to get one, but Victoria seemed to be in a hurry, so I promised myself to do it on the way back and hastily followed her.

We crossed another street, passed a fresh meat and vegetable market, and found a tram stop. I was slightly out of breath from the rushed walk and sat down on the bench to rest. We waited barely three minutes before a tram showed up. Hopping on, we made our way to the front, where we found two seats together.

Jen Tai

Jen Tai's clinic was in an old part of Hong Kong that was quite a distance from the high-rise buildings and skyscrapers of the central business district, so we knew we were in for a long ride. As we sat on the hard wooden seats, we alternated between making conversation and looking out the window. The tram wound its way through the narrow streets, passing a multitude of architectural styles, colorful signs written in Cantonese, and throngs of people jostling each other on their way to life's adventures. I loved riding the tram. It reminded me of my childhood. I liked that it was slow and made frequent stops, and I was starting to get a bit anxious about meeting Jen Tai and what she would say and do. I tried to distract myself with the sights and sounds outside the tram window, focusing on anything that might take my mind to a more positive place.

I watched as a group of kids played football (or soccer, as it's known in the U.S.) in the street with a ball made out of rags tightly wound with string. I marveled at their physical dexterity as they kicked the ball over and through the other kids while dodging cars, pedestrians, and bicycles. But even these young potential Pelés couldn't quell my anxiety.

When we finally hopped off the tram, Victoria led me to an old low-rise building with arched windows. Jen Tai's clinic was on the second floor, and since the building had no elevator, we climbed a set of dark, narrow stairs that creaked and swayed under our weight. The smell of brewing Chinese herbs soon met us, drawing us down a long corridor and through a large, arched wooden door. I was mesmerized by the walls, which were lined with jar after jar of every kind of herb and medicine imaginable: deer horn, sea horses, dandelion tea, and more.

We sat on one of the wooden benches arranged in neat rows, where people waited their turn to go in and consult Jen Tai. I fidgeted a bit, not sure what I had gotten myself into. I studied all the jars on the walls, wondering what magic they might contain.

"These people come from all over Hong Kong, and they all wait to see Jen Tai," Victoria whispered. I could tell that Jen Tai had no shortage of clients, even though she didn't take appointments. It was walk-in only. When our turn finally came, a rather small lady with a very kind and gentle face stuck her head out from behind a wooden door and invited us, in Cantonese, to come in.

As we entered the room where Jen Tai worked, I noticed that her gray hair was pulled back in a tight bun. She wore loose-fitting, comfortable silk clothes. I liked her immediately and felt much more relaxed when I saw her. She smiled at me and asked whether I could speak Cantonese. When I answered her in her native language, her smile grew even wider, and her eyes twinkled.

Victoria started telling Jen Tai about my history with cancer and that I had been stressed recently with work and moving. As Victoria continued, I could see Jen Tai's face start to display a mixture of horror, empathy, and fear. I had been hoping Victoria wouldn't go into all that. I wanted Jen Tai to treat me without having any preconceived impressions.

Jen Tai asked me to stick my tongue out, and she studied it. Then she checked my eyes, looked at my hands, felt my palms, and took my pulse. She asked me to lie down on a cot as she put her fingers on a few different acupressure points on my body. The worried look still hadn't left her face. She retrieved a cloth bag from a cupboard on the side of the bed, and out of the bag she pulled what looked like a black, horn-shaped device with a rounded surface. She pressed the rounded side of the implement against the center of my chest. It felt almost as though she was pushing all the air out of my lungs. She asked me to turn around and then pressed her tool into my back.

"I'm getting the *chi* that is stuck in your chest to move and circulate," she explained. After she finished poking and prodding, she looked at me with genuine kindness as she said, "You need to come back three times a week."

Then she prescribed a series of Chinese herbs and remedies, some of which I would need to boil and drink several times a day. Because I had a history of cancer, she said she wanted to provide me with everything my body needed so that I would not get sick again. I completely trusted her good intentions, but when she said I had to come three times a week, I immediately felt a little ball of stress building in the pit of my stomach. Her clinic was such a long way from my home, and I was still feeling pressure not only from the move but also from the work projects that were piling up.

How could I ever fit in three visits here a week? I thought. *Not to mention the time it's going to take me to prepare the daily regimen of concoctions and potions.*

I asked if perhaps I could come once a week as long as I continued to take the medicines. I explained that it took a huge part of my day just to get to her clinic and back, and there'd be no telling how long the wait would be on any given day.

"It's up to you," Jen Tai replied. "But if your health is important to you, then you need to come more often. The more often you come for treatment, the better for you," she said.

"For how long?" I asked.

"I suggest you consider it part of your weekly routine. It would be beneficial for you to do this for life," she said, with no promise at all of any end point. "Consider it a change in lifestyle."

Herbs and Spices

Do I really have to come for life? I thought, more than slightly panicked. Although I didn't like hearing this, I knew that Jen Tai wasn't deliberately trying to manipulate me. She genuinely believed what she was saying to be true and wanted to help me prevent my cancer from ever recurring. I couldn't expect her to know that the worst thing anyone could do for me would be to suggest I spend the rest of my life continuing to work on keeping cancer at bay. Focusing like that has the exact opposite effect because it just keeps me stuck in the "fear of cancer" paradigm. This is exactly where I was before I even had cancer in the first place.

I have since learned that the healthiest thing I could do was to focus on what brings me joy, to follow my passion, and to make my choices from a place of love, not fear. However, I had temporarily forgotten this, and I found myself getting drawn once more into the world of fear and illness. This experience was now sending me back to my old belief that my body did not have the wisdom to take care of itself without my constant attempts to work on myself and seek intervention from outside experts.

Jen Tai then scribbled some words on a pad of paper, tore off the sheet, and handed it to me, pointing me in the direction of an adjacent room. Following her gesture, I found a young man sitting behind a large wooden counter, about the size of an average dining-room table, mixing potions. I handed him the piece of paper Jen Tai had filled with Chinese writing. He smiled and nodded a thank you.

He then measured and filled several plastic bags with a mixed selection of dried herbs, picking them from this jar and that and weighing them on his handheld scale. Some of the ingredients looked like seeds, others like tree bark, and still others like dried fruit and tea leaves. Each bag held one day's worth of medicine to be boiled in water for four hours before drinking. When he was done, he handed me three bags—three days' worth of medicines. Obviously, Jen Tai was expecting me back within three days. Since I wasn't sure I could make the journey again so soon, I asked him if I could purchase a few more. He was surprised by my Cantonese and broke out into a wide smile. A lively conversation ensued, with both of us smiling and laughing. He provided me with seven bags of ingredients for the medicinal potion, plus a jar of pills, instructing me to take four each day.

After Victoria was done with her consultation and had picked up her own bags of ingredients, we each paid for our potions and our visit and headed back down the narrow stairs and onto the street to look for the nearest tram stop.

"Why did you get so many bags?" Victoria asked me, looking at the seven packets of medicinal herbs.

"Because I'm not sure I can come back three times a week," I told her, "but I do want to keep taking the potion even when I can't visit."

"I don't think it's a good idea for you to miss a visit," Victoria scolded. "Jen Tai really works magic. Did you see how many people wait in line to see her? She is so popular that there must be something to what she does!"

"Yes, I guess you're right," I said, although something still didn't quite feel right. Even so, I wanted to give it a chance because I, too, liked Jen Tai and wanted to benefit from her wisdom.

Taking My Power Back

That evening, I boiled my potion. The fragrance of the herbs permeated our home and wafted out of the front door. When Danny came home, he asked what was cooking, thinking I was making an exotic Chinese soup. I showed him the boiling pot of herbs and told him about my adventure with Victoria.

Over the next three days, I drank my potions and swallowed my pills. Victoria called me on the third day and asked if I wanted to return to Jen Tai's with her. I accepted her invitation, and we again traveled by ferry and tram together. I went with her once more three days after that, then three times again the following week. Jen Tai was always lovely and happy to see me.

Then I got really busy with a new work project. I was tiring of the ordeal of getting to Jen Tai's clinic. It felt like an unnecessary added stress, which was ironic considering that the point was to relieve my tiredness, not to add to it. Besides, I was excited about this new project, and I wanted to dive in. So when Victoria called about our next visit to Jen Tai, I told her I couldn't go.

"I'm feeling fine," I said to her encouragingly. "I just want to focus on things I want to do with my life, not to mention spend some time in my new home." It had started to feel like my life had been revolving around my visits to Jen Tai. I had begun to resent the four-plus hours it took for each round-trip visit, not to mention the time it took to boil up the potions, when I could be listening to my music, reading, going for a walk to the beach, or relaxing instead.

As much as Victoria and Jen Tai insisted that the more often I went, the better I would feel, the exact opposite was happening. The more I went to Jen Tai's, the more I felt I was missing out on everything else I could be doing. Although I'd told Victoria I felt fine, I actually felt *worse* than I did before I started this routine. I also believed that this is why Jen Tai had not yet noticed any improvements in my stress situation. The visits themselves were tiring me out and causing more stress. They were having the opposite effect of what they were supposed to have. Yet Victoria's and Jen Tai's words still triggered a bit of fear within me that made it hard for me to stop going.

"I don't think it's wise to skip visits! She's really helping you!" Victoria implored in an alarmed tone.

"But what if I don't believe that I need help?" I almost said, but I bit my tongue. Instead I responded, "But Victoria, for how long?

She said she wants me to come on a long-term basis! I'm not sure I want to spend such a big part of my life doing that! Not to mention the fact that it's going to cost a lot of money!"

"Anita, you of all people should know that you can't measure health with money!" Victoria retorted. "Besides, Jen Tai is very ethical. She could charge more for what she does if she wanted to, but she doesn't. She has kept her prices the same for a long time. I have been going to her for years, and so have many of her clients. They swear by her and feel that she is a miracle worker. She totally senses what your body needs when she is working on you."

"Yes, Jen Tai is lovely and very empathic. I do see that. But what would you do if you were traveling and couldn't see her regularly? Or if you decided to leave Hong Kong and live somewhere else?" I asked.

"The thought of that worries me sometimes," Victoria admitted. "I feel awful when I can't get to see her for some reason. I am at my best when I go regularly and take all the medicines. And that's my point. She's clearly helping me."

Although something still didn't sit right with me, I didn't want to argue with Victoria. I respected the fact that she believed in Jen Tai, and I didn't want to challenge her beliefs. I know from experience that when we are invested in our beliefs, we can feel a great deal of fear when others shatter them—unless those shattered beliefs are replaced by a new, more empowering possibility. I felt as though I were in a lose-lose situation—if I stopped going, I might not be doing what was best for my health and my body; but if I kept going, I'd continue to feel frustrated, stressed, and even fearfully dependent on Jen Tai.

Victoria had completely given her power away to the healer, and the thought of not seeing her for treatments for any length of time made Victoria afraid. She seemed to believe that her body did not have the wisdom to maintain health without constant and continual intervention. Although I couldn't see it at that time, the truth was that I, too, was starting to lose my personal power to Jen Tai.

Rebellion

That evening, I decided to spend some time alone in quiet meditation. I needed to tune in to myself and hear what guidance I could find there. I got into comfy clothes, lit some candles, warmed up my favorite aromatherapy oils, and played some soft music. Then I sat on a few cushions, gazing out toward the ocean. The music had a mesmerizing effect on me, as did the lovely fragrance of the oils. I kept focusing on the ocean as I completely relaxed, letting all my thoughts just drift away.

I have learned that if I focus on something vast, like the ocean, not paying attention to any stray thoughts that try to intrude, after a while I drop into a deeper state where everything is suddenly clear. With the external noise gone, my wise inner self can communicate with me—and there's no mistaking the messages. The emotions are intense, similar to what I felt during my near-death experience, and sometimes I even feel a corresponding physical sensation.

On this evening, after spending about 20 minutes gazing out through the balcony's glass doors, I suddenly hit this state of clarity. It started out as a physical sensation around my throat, a sort of tingling. I recognized that the sensation was my body's way of announcing that I wasn't expressing my truth right now. I started to bring my awareness into my throat area to see what would come up. Focusing there, I asked whether it had a message for me. Several thoughts came flooding through: *I do not need to depend on external sources to dictate my well-being. I do not need to give my power away to Jen Tai. The more I give my power away, the more I am feeding the belief that there is something fundamentally wrong with me and that I have to rely on others to make decisions for me. I do not need to put the power to make decisions about my health in someone else's hands.*

These truths came in a torrent, as if a floodgate had been opened. I always know when I'm hearing truth from my inner guidance because all the fear disappears and it's replaced with a feeling of joy and lightness. And that's exactly how I felt at that moment.

I realized that the more I believed that Jen Tai held all the power to heal me, the weaker I had become. And this weakness led me to believe that I needed even more help! I don't deny that we often need help from others—be they allopathic physicians, complementary medicine practitioners, or even energy healers. After all, I myself had received much-needed advice and treatment from both medical doctors and Ayurvedic healers when I had cancer. The difference was that I eagerly sought their assistance because it felt like the right thing for me to do at that time—I didn't allow myself to be manipulated into seeing them by others who projected their fear onto me and who thought they knew better than I did what I most needed (even if their intentions were good and their motives pure). It had been my decision and it felt right.

Of course, I'm not saying Jen Tai and other Traditional Chinese Medicine (TCM) practitioners aren't valuable. They certainly are! In fact, I very much respect TCM practitioners and their treatments. When we feel guided to see any kind of practitioner, and when we take herbs and supplements or prescription medications because we want to and it feels good, we're listening to our inner guidance and we're empowering ourselves. These are important steps to facilitate our health and well-being.

In fact, one of the vital differences between a *good* healer and a *great* healer is that a great healer guides you back to your own innate ability to heal and ultimately encourages your independence. Great healers know that we all have an innate wisdom, and they see their job as helping us get in touch with that wisdom. A lot of healers want you to stay dependent on them, even if they don't do it consciously, because this justifies their existence. These healers have often not tapped into their own invincible selves, and so they, too, believe that we all need constant intervention and fixing. Consequently, they project this same belief onto their clients. But a great healer's goal is to empower *you* by creating a channel for you to tap into your own natural healing abilities. This, of course, eventually makes the healer unnecessary. But for a healer, this is the price of greatness!

The same applies with great teachers and great gurus. A really great teacher or guru knows that their true purpose is *not* winning popularity contests by accumulating more and more disciples who are dependent on them for answers. Their true purpose is to awaken the inner guru or wisdom within each of their students, thereby freeing them from the *need* to have a teacher. There's nothing wrong with having teachers, healers, and gurus whom you respect, but when you believe in yourself and are in touch with your own inner guidance system, the right guru, teacher, or healer will come to you at the right time, with the answer you need in that moment. And they can come in any form—even as an electrician, a cab driver, or someone on television. You'll know because what you hear will resonate from deep within you, triggering a feeling of excitement, and the message won't cause anxiety or fear to bubble up.

My experience with Victoria and Jen Tai, as much as I loved them both, taught me that it's completely counterproductive—and harmful—to give my power away. I don't need *constant* fixing for the rest of my life. I used to believe that obsessing about health was healthy, as long as I was working with natural modalities as opposed to taking prescription medications and drugs. But I've since learned that constantly being focused on my health just keeps me trapped in the belief that something is wrong. After all, obsessing about *anything* isn't healthy—even obsessing about health itself—when the underlying motivation is fear, not accessing true guidance.

Living Heaven *Here and Now*

If "Something's wrong with me that needs to be fixed" is a *myth*, then what could be the *truth*?

Consider These Possible Truths

- We are born perfect in every way.

- We are already everything that we are trying to become.

- Although we may have temporarily forgotten who we are, we are not broken in any way!

- The challenges in our lives are not an indication that there's anything wrong with us; instead, they're merely part of the journey back to ourselves.

Tips and Exercises

- Make time each day to tune in to your inner guidance system.

- Be open to guidance of all sorts—the song playing on the car radio when you switch it on, bits of conversation you overhear in line at the supermarket, or an interview you read in a magazine or watch on television.

- Learn to recognize when something you hear triggers a feeling of excitement deep within you—that's your guidance system telling you to pay attention.

- Get in the habit of looking at your challenges as blessings. Instead of getting angry and frustrated when something isn't going the way you would like, ask yourself, *If this were actually a gift from the universe, what would it be here to teach me?* You'll be amazed how that shift in perspective can open you up to wisdom from within.

Questions to Ask Yourself

- Am I constantly obsessed with working on myself, trying to "improve" myself in some way?

- Do I always feel the need to seek external help from books, teachers, or gurus to advise me on how to lead my life?

- Do I give my power away to others by believing that everyone else has the answers I need?

- Am I able to discern when I'm hearing the universe share guidance truly meant for me and when the advice I'm hearing is not actually in my best interest?

- Am I too critical of myself?

I know I am in touch with my inner guidance system when . . .

- I can truly see how the challenges in my life are not due to personal failings but are instead an important part of my journey.

- I recognize that those same challenges are actually gifts.

- I stop feeling an obsessive need to be in control of all of the events around me, as well as of their outcomes.

- I allow myself to be a channel through which life expresses itself, fully recognizing that life happens *through* me, not *to* me.

MYTH:

HEALTH CARE CARES
FOR OUR HEALTH

I was back in Hong Kong after flying all over Europe and North America for speaking engagements. I was really enjoying being home, if only for a few days. I was having a pleasant time at Li Chong's neighborhood grocery store, trying to figure out whether I wanted to buy Gala or Rose apples. *Hmmm* . . . I was thinking, *Do I want Gala or Rose? Rose or Gala?*

Interrupted in my profound ponderings by my mobile phone ringing, I dropped a bag of Rose apples into my shopping cart (I decided I liked the name better) and reached into my handbag for my phone. No name was displayed on the screen—which meant the call wasn't from anyone on my contact list. Nor did I recognize the number.

"Hello?" I said into the phone with some hesitation.

"Hello? Is this Anita?" said an unfamiliar voice.

"Yes, this is Anita. May I ask who's calling?"

"I don't know if you remember me. My name is Vera, and we met once during the conference at the university last year."

"Umm . . . ," I said, wracking my mind to remember, but I couldn't quite place her.

"It's okay, I understand if you don't remember me," she replied, sensing my dilemma. "You must meet a lot of people these days. I really hope you don't mind me calling you out of the blue like this, but I was desperate to talk to you. Are you busy right now? Is this a good time to talk?"

"It's fine. I'm just grocery shopping—nothing very exciting," I said, curious as to how she got my number and why she would call.

As if reading my mind, Vera said, "At the conference, we were introduced by a mutual friend, Sheila Randall. She's the one who gave me your number and suggested I call."

"Ah yes, I remember now! What's up?" I asked, suddenly remembering that my friend Sheila, whom I knew from the yoga classes I used to attend, had introduced me to a very pleasant Eurasian woman at a university conference where I'd spoken the previous year.

It's My Mother . . .

"Well, it's my mother," Vera said, her voice now quavering. "She has breast cancer! She only found out last week, and it's at stage three! She has been feeling so much fear since the diagnosis—as if the doctors have given her a death sentence! Then someone recommended that she read your book, which she did right away. It gave her so much hope. Then when she realized that you live here in Hong Kong, she really wanted to meet you and talk with you. So I contacted Sheila, and she agreed I should call."

"Oh, I'm so sorry to hear about your mother," I responded. "I really feel for her—and for you! I *know* what this journey is like!" I genuinely felt Vera's pain, and I was so touched that my book had helped her mother. "I totally understand how scary it can be to be told you have stage three cancer."

"That's why I called," Vera said, with a little sigh of relief. "When my mother read your story, she felt you were telling *her* story. She is exactly how you used to be! She's a people pleaser,

MYTH: HEALTH CARE CARES FOR OUR HEALTH

giving and giving until she has no more to give. But she never takes care of herself!"

I felt a slight smile form on the corners of my mouth at the thought of how familiar this sounded. It was indeed my story!

"Where is your mother now?" I asked, feeling some trepidation because although I wanted to help, I also wanted Vera's mother to know that she had the power to heal (whatever form that healing might take) already within her. I didn't want her to think that she needed me in order to heal. I share my message not so that others can believe in *me*, but so they can believe in *themselves*.

In addition, I was on a tight schedule, and I'd started receiving lots of requests from people I didn't know who were facing serious illnesses, asking me to visit them and help them through their healing journey. This made me feel really uncomfortable because I genuinely wanted to help *everyone*, but that was, of course, physically impossible. If I could, I would've scooped every single one of them up in my arms and given them all a big hug, asking them to love themselves and accept themselves fully for who they are, wherever they are on their journey!

"She's at the Adventist Hospital on Stubbs Road," Vera answered. "The sooner you can see her, the better, because she is very fearful about the treatment options and completely overwhelmed by all the different advice she's getting." By this point, Vera was speaking through tears.

"I'll clear my schedule tomorrow afternoon to go see her," I told Vera. Even though I was leaving Hong Kong again in three days and hadn't even begun to prepare for the trip, I felt compelled to help Vera and her mother. I just couldn't leave her in this kind of distress, no matter how busy I was—that option just didn't feel right to me. I could feel Vera's fear run right through me like an icy chill, and it made me shiver.

Health Care—or Illness (S)care?

After my experience with cancer, I developed a very different outlook on health and the way we focus on it. It frustrates me that our health-care system places far more emphasis on looking for illness than it does on living a healthy life. We seem to have become obsessed with cancer awareness and are constantly bombarded by ad campaigns encouraging us to go for early detection tests, which only encourages us to focus on illness! We are also continually asked to donate to "the war against cancer," as well as various other "wars" against heart disease, diabetes, and so on.

If we talked about health as much as we talked about cancer, if we poured as much money into health awareness as we do into cancer awareness, we'd very likely have a very different reality. This is why I love to talk about health, love, and joy instead of putting attention on cancer. I would love to see people have more dialogues about what it takes to be healthy, what healthy looks like, and what health feels like. Even those suffering from cancer would benefit from this!

I want to be crystal clear about this: Our bodies are *not* war zones, and we must stop treating them as if they were. There are no battles to be won—or lost—and no enemies to destroy. Getting cancer or any other illness can either be a gift or a curse, depending on how we look at it. These diseases are not "evils that need to be wiped out." They are not the result of "bad karma from a past life," nor are they the result of our negative thoughts.

Rather, illness is our body's way of communicating with us and showing us a better path. Yes, we may die from cancer—or from countless other things—and each of us *will die* from something at some point. But death is not the enemy. What often *is* the enemy is the way we view illness, including the simplistic notion that if we get sick or die, it's because we didn't fight long or hard enough, we weren't brave enough, we didn't have a strong enough will to live, or that our thoughts and visualizations were not positive enough. These notions not only cause fear, they are also *simply not true*! And they demean the person who is caught up in the health challenge, putting tremendous pressure on them—and their loved ones—when they're at their most vulnerable.

This judgmental, unfair attitude is *just the opposite* of the love, support, and understanding that anyone going through such an event needs. Imagine how much more helpful it would be to change our focus and see cancer and other illnesse. *calls* to shift our life path. What if instead of spendii of dollars waging war against disease, we put the sam. of money, energy, and focus into spreading health-awaren ,.o-grams covering not only our physical health but also our mental, emotional, and spiritual health? Think about what a difference that would make and what a different outcome we would have!

Health Awareness

Our health-care system, as it stands now, is really an illness-care program dedicated more to disease than to health—perhaps partly because there's much more money to be made from illness than wellness. Some would say I'm just being cynical, but consider this: In 2014, *Forbes* reported that the amount spent in the U.S. on doctors, hospitals, medications, and therapy is estimated to be $3.8 trillion. Compared to such a massive outlay, we spend a mere pittance educating people on the best ways to live a longer, happier, and healthier life.

According to Lyle Ungar, Ph.D., professor of computer and information science at the University of Pennsylvania who has done extensive work on life expectancy and has also helped create a life-expectancy calculator, we can all live longer and healthier simply by not smoking, not driving drunk, wearing a seat belt, exercising more, and cultivating meaningful relationships. That's it. We could save tons of money and millions of lives a year just by following these simple guidelines.

Most people don't really know what true wellness is. They have no idea that their physical well-being has a *lot* to do with their mental, emotional, and spiritual well-being! It's all tied together—physical illness does not happen in a vacuum. Our immune system becomes depleted, making us more susceptible to illness, for a *reason*. Until health-care specialists start to focus on health instead of illness, and until researchers look deeper into the connection between disease and our emotions and lifestyle, we will not find cures in medical research alone.

Unfortunately for Vera's mother, she was already enrolled in the illness system. It was time to take a different approach.

Meeting Dana

The day after my conversation with Vera, I knocked on the door of her mother's hospital room. She'd undergone a biopsy two days prior, but the doctors had more tests to run.

"Come in," I heard Vera call out, so I slowly opened the door and stepped into the room. Vera and her mother both looked relieved and happy to see me.

"Thank you so much for coming! I know how busy you are!" Vera said as she got out of her seat and moved a chair from the other side of the room so I could sit next to her.

"It's quite all right," I answered. "I'm very happy I can be here with you."

"Meet my mother, Dana," Vera said, gently placing her hand on her mother's arm as she spoke. Dana was smiling, and although she had a lovely face, she looked so pale lying there with IV tubes in her arms. She looked far too young to have a daughter of Vera's age. I decided she must have had her very early in her adult life.

"Hi, Dana," I said, smiling as I sat down.

"I'm so glad you came to see me," Dana replied. "I was so excited when Vera said you would visit. I just finished reading your book, and it was very helpful."

"How are you feeling?" I asked.

"Frightened and confused!" she answered. "I find hospitals scary for a start. Everyone is so serious here, and that makes me feel even more unwell."

"I know *exactly* what you mean," I said, looking around at the stark white walls, the hard plastic and metal chairs, and the overall clinical atmosphere of the place. "You'd think they would paint the walls in beautiful bright colors; hang up happy pictures of cuddly puppy dogs, flowers, and rainbows; and wear colorful clothes to cheer up the patients, wouldn't you?"

I didn't even mention the fashion faux pas that is the patient's hospital gown! No garment on this earth is less dignified! Surely modifying these outfits can't be all that difficult—even just adding little touches to make the patient experience a bit more pleasant. It's no wonder that when I was dealing with my own cancer, I just hated staying in the hospital. I would insist on going home each time after treatment, no matter how awful I felt, simply because I felt even *worse* staying in the hospital!

The Glut of Information

"The doctors have outlined several options, and I am so scared," Dana continued. "My oncologist says I'd be crazy not to go with chemotherapy and that it's my only chance. But I'm frightened by the gruesome side effects. And the naturopath I've been seeing, a man I really trust, insists that chemo poisons our bodies.

"On top of that, my friends and family all have different opinions about what I should do. Some don't agree with my doctors and print information about alternative cures off the Internet for me. Others warn me to stick to my doctors' advice and ignore everything else. Still others assure me that God will heal me if I just have enough faith. All the conflicting advice makes me feel almost paralyzed. It's more than I can deal with. Don't get me wrong—these are all well-meaning people who love me. But now I feel that no matter *what* I do, I might be making the wrong choice."

I could tell by Dana's exasperated tone and the expression on her face that she truly did feel paralyzed—afraid to take a step in any direction, as if she were surrounded by land mines without a map, or worse, with several conflicting maps!

I also felt a sense of déjà vu as Dana spoke. I'd dealt with these same issues during my own bout with cancer. I'd been bombarded with facts and opinions, and instead of gaining clarity from them, I'd felt overwhelmed and afraid because so much of the information was conflicting. The more I researched, the more contradictory information I found.

"What would *you* choose in this situation, Anita?" Dana asked.

"I'm hesitant to give you specific advice, Dana, because you need to own your decisions and recognize your ability to create your own path. I don't want you giving that power to me," I said. "Also, if I just gave you advice, I'd only be adding to the glut of confusing information you already have. It would serve you much better to feel empowered. Right now, it's about you and no one else. However, I'm willing to guide you as you go inward to see how these options feel to you so you can start to make some choices."

"I'd really appreciate that," she said, looking much more hopeful than when I had arrived.

The Inner Voice Speaks

"I know I'm led all the time by a kind of inner guidance system—something I believe we *all* have that is *always* trying to communicate with us," I explained. "But when we're overloaded with conflicting information, our minds get so frazzled that our guidance system finds it hard to communicate with us. With the speed that information is now available to us today, this overload occurs frequently. When that happens to me, I go on an information fast."

"What's that?" Dana asked with great interest.

"Just as when people go on a food fast where they don't eat anything for 24 to 48 hours, an information fast involves not taking in any new information from the outside world for at least a day or two—longer if possible," I responded. "When I stop overwhelming my mind, I can start to hear my inner guidance system speaking to me."

"Tell me more about this guidance system. Where is the information coming from?" Dana asked.

"I sense it coming from everywhere and nowhere at the same time," I answered. "I know that I exist beyond my body—I learned that during my near-death experience. In that state, I was limitless and connected to everyone and everything in the universe. There was no separation. Now that I'm back in the physical world, these fasts help me to remember that I'm still connected, including to loved ones who have passed on—my father and my best friend, Soni, for example. I sense my guidance coming from them, and I know that there are others, too, who love me unconditionally and watch over me, helping me in this world. Knowing this brings me great comfort and peace.

"When I said that there's no separation and that we're connected, that includes being connected to those from other time periods, because as I learned in the other realm, there is no time as we know it there. That means your guidance could be coming from your deceased loved ones or from others who lived before you such as Jesus, Buddha, Shiva, Kwan Yin, or any other beings you feel a special connection with—even from someone who from our linear perspective hasn't even been born yet!

"It's actually not relevant who your guides are because they're all connected to us as one, presenting themselves in our mind's eye in whatever form we feel most comfortable with. I know this might sound strange, but I feel guided whenever I tune in and remember not to give my power away to all the external noise."

"I used to feel guided when I was younger," Dana said excitedly, "but I've lost that feeling over the years!"

"That's the case with most of us," I told her. "I think we're born with that capacity, but we lose it as we go through life and begin listening to all the conflicting voices around us. Somehow, life seems to strip us of our own power!"

Vera had been quiet through most of the conversation, but I could tell she was listening intently, taking everything in. I really wanted to help her support her mother through this. They had such a beautiful relationship. When I had cancer, Danny and the rest of my family never left my side. Support like that is vital, and I was glad that Dana could count on her daughter.

"So right now," Dana said, "it would serve me to go on an information fast so that my mind can be clear of clutter and my internal guidance system can start to communicate with me directly. Is that what you would suggest?"

"Yes, that's what I would do!" I said. Now it was my turn to be excited. "Basically, when I feel confused and overwhelmed with information, I don't go looking for more of it. I just kind of let the information I already have settle. I cannot un-know any of the information I already have, of course, so I just let it be without specifically focusing on any of it."

Choosing Joy

"Then," I continued, "I tell myself that I need to focus on making choices that support my body, my spirit, and my personal journey. Focusing on doing what makes me happy—instead of on cancer—moves me from the fear-feeling place of thinking, *Oh my God, I have cancer, now what do I have to do to get rid of it?* to a place of peace and being grounded.

"If I were to find myself back in the fear-feeling place where I am having thoughts like, *What if I choose the wrong thing?* I would not try to force the fears out, because I would only end up fearing the fear and judging it every time it surfaces. I would just let the fears be, while at the same time gently introducing a new line of thinking, telling myself something like this: *Okay, Anita, it's time to reclaim my happiness. It's time to spend some time on myself, loving myself, being gentle and kind to myself, and taking care of myself by doing something fun and interesting.*"

"I need to take notes," Dana suddenly said. "Vera, will you please grab my notepad and pen from my purse?" Vera rummaged through Dana's bag and handed a diary and pen to her mother.

"I'd also ask myself questions like, *How can I love myself more? How can I support myself more? What would I be doing if I did love myself? What can I do each day to show myself how much I love and support myself?*" I continued. "And then I would write down what comes to me and actually do these things each day. I would also ask myself, *What would I do today to celebrate my good health if I found out that I was completely healed and totally cancer free?* and then I'd go out and do it! I think it's important to celebrate life each and every day, and sometimes it takes getting an illness to remind us to do that!

"I've also learned that it's important to feel that what I'm doing comes from a place of love and not from a place of fear,"

I added. "That is, I make whatever choice I make because I love myself, treasure my life, and want to feel good again—not because I fear what will happen otherwise. Not only is this more empowering, but positive outcomes are *much* more likely."

Fear-Based Medicine

"I totally get what you are saying, Anita, and I completely agree with you," Dana said as she put down her pen and took a sip of water. "It makes me feel so much better hearing this from you. But you know what's hard? Dealing with the doctors, because they keep me in a state of fear. They feel this obligation to be 'realistic,' and they want to tell me the statistics and base my prognosis on them. I wish they understood that I don't *want* to know worst-case scenarios! I don't consider myself a statistic. I'm an individual, and I can be my *own* statistic!"

I knew exactly what Dana was saying. The same fear-based options and statistics were presented to me during my own illness. The tragically ironic point of this is that skeptics often confront me, claiming that my ideas on health are dangerous because they give people a false sense of security and steer them away from the harsh reality of their disease. But from my perspective, it's the fear surrounding the dictums of the medical practitioners that contributes to the danger. Fear does tremendous damage to our immune system, leaving us vulnerable to disease.

Medical practitioners are well aware of the power of suggestibility, and the placebo effect has been studied for many years, starting with Dr. Henry Beecher's groundbreaking clinical review entitled "The Powerful Placebo," published in the *Journal of the American Medical Association* in 1955.

Despite knowing this, our medical practitioners not only do nothing to counteract fear in their patients, but many seem to intentionally *instill* fear. This is confirmed by the volume of e-mails I receive daily from people dealing with a grim prognosis given to them by an intimidating practitioner, not to mention an intimidating medical system. They write asking whether

I have any advice on overcoming this fear as they walk through this emotional minefield. That was also my experience when I had cancer. I hated going to the doctor's office because being there made me feel more fearful. I felt even sicker when I was in the hospital, while I always felt much better at home.

"I hear you, Dana," I replied. "Isn't it ironic that the very institutions we have created for our healing and well-being are the places we inadvertently fear most because the information—as well as the treatments—are presented in a cold, clinical, and fearful way? These 'health-care' institutions seem to actually compound our illness!"

"*Yes!*" Dana answered vehemently. "We are treated like mechanical beings with very little regard for us as individuals!"

Love, Not Fear

Since my own illness, I have felt strongly that when someone is diagnosed with any life-threatening illness, the focus needs to be not just on the person's physical state, but also on their emotional state—perhaps even more so! Ideally, their health-care provider would ask questions like these:

- Do you love and value yourself?
- Are you happy?
- Are there people in your life who matter to you and to whom you matter?
- Do you feel your life has purpose?
- What are you passionate about?
- What brings you joy?

"Okay," Dana said, "Let's say I'm now acting from a place of love, spending more time doing things that nourish and nurture me and connecting with people who support me. And so then I get to a place where I feel empowered and in tune with my guidance system, but I still have to make some hard choices for treatment options. How would I ask my guidance system which choice to make?"

"Great question!" I said. "I would start to pull up all the various treatment options that I have been presented with, and then check in on how each of the choices makes me feel. For example, I'd ask myself, *How do I feel when I think of chemotherapy?* Then I'd observe whether that scenario makes me feel as if I'd be putting poisons into my body, like your naturopath suggests, or whether I see it as something powerful that would help me eradicate the cancer cells. Then I'd ask, *How do I feel when I think of the suggestions the naturopath has outlined for me? How does it feel to do a combination, so that I can eradicate the cancer cells with chemotherapy and support my body with good nutrition at the same time? Do I feel hopeful or fearful when I think about a faith-based approach? How do I feel about a combination of all three?*

"If there were more than one naturopathic, oncological, or faith-based choice, I'd think of each of them in turn, each time asking myself, *How does this choice make me feel? Do I feel strong and empowered at the thought of a life journey with this option, or does considering it make me fearful and weak? How do I feel about death itself? Am I filled with a sense of dread, or am I at peace with death, seeing it as a natural course for life to take?*

"In each case, I'd observe what emotions each option triggers, and then I would go with the choices that make me feel the most empowered, the most hopeful, the happiest. And I wouldn't worry whether my choices would offend those who are supporting me because truly, each of us needs to be surrounded by those who love us, empower us, and will support our choices. After all, your life and your health are about *you*."

"Wow, that is so helpful!" Dana said.

"Exactly the same applies with diet and nutrition," I added. "There's so much contradicting information about what is and what is not good for us. I used to be so anxious about everything I ate. I was vegan for two years because a naturopath I knew swore by that diet and convinced me animal protein caused cancer. But I became malnourished as a result, which caused a whole lot of other health problems. When I started this method of checking in with my body, my health improved drastically. For example, I soon realized that I was extremely low on protein. So I started eating eggs, and then fish, and I felt better immediately!

"Certain things are common sense, like eating good-quality, whole foods while avoiding processed foods, particularly when our health is compromised. But I don't think there's one single diet or way of eating that fits everyone. To advocate a particular diet as the one and only way just puts those who don't follow that way into fear. My decision to be vegan was made out of fear, specifically fear of cancer; I didn't make that decision out of love for my body. And of course I *did* end up getting cancer, so any benefit I might have received from eating vegan was compromised by all the stress hormones my body was pumping out from living in a constant state of low-level fear. If I had instead loved my body and truly wanted to do everything I could to have a joyful life, I would have tuned in to discover how my body actually needed to be nourished. But that didn't occur to me because I was spending all my energy on being anxious and afraid.

"This doesn't mean that I don't go for medical or natural intervention when I need it," I clarified. "I certainly believe that when we need support, we must seek it out. But I now feel that the intervention must empower us, not strip us of our power. That's the difference. And the way to know is to check in with yourself.

"By the way," I added, "I use this method with just about every choice I make these days, including deciding which speaking engagement to accept if the dates overlap, or even whether to accept a new project. Before I commit to anything, I imagine myself in each situation, and then I accept only the ones that bring me a feeling of joy, passion, or purpose—the ones that make me happiest.

"Most of us are taught to evaluate choices by analyzing with our minds, like making lists of the pros and cons for each choice, and then choosing the option with the longest list of pros. But even if you go with that, how do you *feel* doing it? Does it make your heart sing? Does it fill you with passion? Or are you filled instead with anxiety, waiting for it to be over, instead of looking forward to doing it?"

"What you say makes a lot of sense to me!" Dana exclaimed. "I so agree with you. Making more heart-based decisions sounds like such a great idea! But don't you find yourself constantly being pulled back into your head because most people around us don't think like that? Somehow, the environment we live in seems to demand that we function purely from our logical mind."

"All the time!" I replied. "Even after the incredible experience I had with my NDE, I still feel as though the world around me demands that I deny what my inner guidance tells me is the truth of how to live. It seems I'm constantly in a position of having to choose to either fit in with everyone else or live my truth and be an outsider. I can't usually have it both ways!"

"And I thought *I* was the only one who felt that way!" Dana cried out. "One of the hardest things for me right now is all the conflicting advice I'm getting from well-meaning people who love me. I know that no matter what I decide, I can only take the advice of some of them and will be going against the advice of others. I'm finding that challenging."

Ignoring the "Shoulds"

It was unbelievable how much of my previous self I could see in Dana, and I now understood why I had felt pulled to come and meet with her. I, too, used to be such a people pleaser. In fact, wanting to please others so they will like me still rears its head from time to time and forces me to actively assess every interaction. In the past, much of my life was dictated by what others thought of me. Talking with Dana felt like looking into a mirror and seeing the personality I had before my NDE.

"I used to feel exactly the same way, Dana," I responded empathically. "But what I've learned is that when people say that I should do this or that, they may be speaking from their *own* place of fear. What they are really saying without realizing it is that this is what *they* would do if they were in my situation, and so it would bring *them* peace of mind if I took their advice.

"What works for me in these situations is to thank them for their advice and for their caring, and to let them know that I will consider what they've offered, along with all the other information I have. But I then ask them to fully support me in whatever I finally choose, even if it's different from what they advised. I know that I would not make them feel obligated to follow my advice if they were in my situation, so I deserve the same in return. And you know what? In most cases, people who really care about me will support my choices. They don't always realize the pressure they're exerting, and once they become aware of that, they ease off."

"You cannot imagine how happy I am to hear you tell her this, Anita!" Vera chimed in. "Mom is always trying to please everyone, and she worries she might lose people's support if she has to go against their advice."

"In that case, I'm glad I brought it up too!" I responded. "If you're going to lose anyone's support because you want to follow your own heart, then they aren't the right person to support you through this journey! It's so important that the people you have around you right now support you for who you are, not because you are doing what they say.

"By the way," I added, "I think the two of you are so lucky to have each other."

"Yes, I really do feel blessed to have Vera in my life!" Dana agreed, taking a moment to give her daughter a loving glance. From the look Vera gave her mother in return, it was obvious the feeling was mutual.

Glancing at the clock on the wall, I suddenly realized it was much later than I thought.

"Oh my, is that the time?" I asked. "I had no idea! I'm afraid I'll have to run!" I leaned over the bed and gave Dana a hug as I said good-bye. For someone who had initially looked so weak, she gave me a tight hug that felt strong and loving.

"Thank you so much for stopping by!" Dana said. "It meant a lot to me, and I'll treasure everything we spoke about! You have no idea how much you have helped me today." Tears were welling up in her eyes, and I could feel them starting to prickle my own eyes, as well.

"Stay strong and never forget who you are," I said as I slowly pulled myself away from her, turning to pick up my handbag.

"I will," she responded, holding her hand to her heart. Vera saw me out of the hospital to the taxi queue, and I felt so much warmth in her gratitude.

"I haven't seen my mom look this happy in a long while!" she said with a grin as I climbed into the cab. "Thank you for giving her something so positive to focus on!"

"Seeing you and your mother made my day! You both really warm my heart!" I told her just before shutting the car door. I waved at her as the taxi turned the corner and made its way to the pier, where I would catch my ferry home.

On the ride back across Victoria Harbor to Discovery Bay, I savored the time I had spent with Vera and Dana, reliving our conversation in my mind. It was hard to know what Dana's outcome would be. Would she find a healing path to restored vigor and life, or would she pass into the world beyond this one—a world I knew well from my own experience? Whatever the outcome, I knew *the journey itself* was the most important part. After our visit, I felt confident that her path would veer away from fear and trepidation and would instead be one of love and joy, and that she would seek out those people and activities that would best support her along the way.

I also thought about my own journey and realized again how difficult it often is to stay centered on what brings me the most peace and joy—even when I know exactly what that is. But I knew that in the case of my visit that afternoon, the impulse to go see Dana hadn't come from a place of needing to please others but from a true inner sense that going to see her would be the choice that would make me the happiest, increasing my own sense of joy and well-being. And that's *exactly* how it turned out to be!

Living Heaven *Here and Now*

If "The health-care system takes care of our health" is a *myth*, then what could be the *truth*?

Consider These Possible Truths

- Doctors and other health-care professionals can give us information about our physical condition and what our options are, but we are responsible for accessing our guidance and deciding on the best course of action.

- Poor health is not only a medical issue; the causes can also be rooted in our mental, emotional, or spiritual state—as well as in our environment.

- We are not victims of illness because illness and disease do not happen in a vacuum; we can do much to improve our health on many levels.

- Illness is a teacher—and often a wake-up call—that shows us a better path. It's not an evil that must be destroyed, the consequence of bad karma, or the result of negative thinking. Even death itself is not our enemy.

- Choosing to see the gifts or messages in illness instead of viewing illness as a curse empowers us (and may very well improve the outcome of an illness).

Tips and Exercises

- If you or a loved one develop an illness that continues to progress, resist any temptation to believe the sick person did something wrong to cause the disease or did not do enough to fight it off. Recognize these thoughts for what they are—unfair and harmful judgments. Instead, surround yourself or your loved one with support, understanding, and love.

- The next time you experience information overload of any sort, consider going on an information fast: Don't take in any new information from the outside world for at least a day or two to make it easier for you to hear the promptings from your internal guidance system.

- Learn to access your guidance system anytime you need to make a choice. As you consider each option, pay attention to what emotions it triggers and how it makes you feel (hopeful and empowered versus fearful and weak). Go with the best-feeling option.

- If you have trouble accessing your true feelings about a choice, try flipping a coin. Notice your gut reaction to the outcome of the toss—if you feel a positive response, go with that option. If your gut clenches, choose a different option.

- When fear threatens to overwhelm you, focus on doing what makes you happy instead of focusing on what you fear. This will help to move you to a state of peace and being grounded where you can more easily access your guidance.

- When others are insistent about what they think you should do, realize they are talking from their *own* place of fear. Sincerely thank them for their love and caring, and then ask them to support whatever decision you finally choose—even if it's not what they want you to do.

- If your doctor proposes a treatment course that sounds overwhelming or scary, ask what they would prescribe if one of their own family members or a loved one had this same diagnosis.

- If instead of telling you that you are healed, your doctor tells you that you are in remission (a word that I personally dislike because it disempowers you), tell yourself that you are *done* with cancer. Think of the word "remission" as "remembering my mission." It's now time to embrace life and remember your mission!

Questions to Ask Yourself

- As I look at past illnesses or injuries, what connections can I make between my physical condition and my mental, emotional, or spiritual health at the time?

- If a past illness was truly a wake-up call to shift my life path in some way, what changes might my body have been prompting me to make?

- Do I feel more anxious discussing my condition and treatment options with some people compared to others? If so, am I open to making the decision not to have these discussions with these people, even if they mean well?

- What can I do today to show myself how much I love and support myself? And what can I do tomorrow and the day after that?

- How could I truly celebrate life today—what life-affirming activity could I take part in— regardless of my physical state?

I know I am taking responsibility for my own health when . . .

- I welcome information from both health-care professionals and friends and family members with gratitude for their expertise and concern, without feeling overwhelmed or obligated to take any particular course of action offered.

- I can access my guidance system to assess what feels right for me at any given time, as opposed to letting fear influence my decisions.

- I recognize my body as a barometer for the state of my mental, emotional, and spiritual health (along with my physical health), and I am grateful for its lessons and its guidance.

MYTH:
IT'S JUST A COINCIDENCE

Flying back and forth from my home city of Hong Kong to the U.S. was really starting to wear on both Danny and me. As much as we enjoy travel, adventure, and seeing new places, we were beginning to feel that we were spending far too much time sitting on airplanes, waiting at airports, standing in queues, and going through security. And when we weren't flying, we were dealing with jet lag as a result of crossing multiple time zones. So finally, in January 2015, we took the plunge and made the move from Hong Kong to the U.S. We chose to live in Southern California, mainly because I like being by the ocean and we are used to mild weather.

A New and Unsettling Reality

We both love being in the U.S., and we love California—but one aspect of our new environment hit me strongly. Danny often turns on the television to watch the news while getting dressed in the morning. This never used to bother me when we were living in Hong Kong because the news there is not all that exciting or intrusive. It's mostly reports of our government's meetings with the governments of neighboring cities like Beijing or Taiwan.

What struck me about news in the U.S., though, was the amount of violent crime reported every day. In Asia, there were rarely any violent crimes to report. Guns are pretty much nonexistent in most Asian cultures, but in the U.S., each day I was hearing reports of mindless killings taking place in schools, churches, theaters, and private homes. These were just normal people going about their day being killed in the most bloody, violent ways imaginable! Often the victims were children, and many of the deaths seemed racially driven.

This was quite a shock to my spirit, affecting me emotionally and psychologically. I asked Danny to please keep the television turned off so we could play uplifting music instead. And while he readily complied, something in the back of my mind kept nagging at me. Even though I could start my day with music, I knew these shootings were still going on. Just because I didn't turn on my television didn't mean the violence wasn't happening. I realized that all I was doing was burying my head in the sand.

Duality Versus Non-duality

The reason hearing these sensational news stories affects me so much is that I know that we are all connected, yet we are killing each other and spreading hatred because we are ignorant of this interconnection. We aren't aware that we are hurting our own brothers and sisters, our own children, our own parents . . . our own selves! The belief that we are separate from everyone else is a major cause of wars throughout the world. We train our young adults to go to war and kill people (often other young people) who live in another nation just because their government leaders don't agree with ours. And then we celebrate those who kill the most— or who save others on their side from being killed—as war heroes. Both killing and saving are two sides of the same coin. If we eliminated the killing, we would have no need for saving.

What I realized when I died was that those we kill are not separate from us. Imagine that we're like fingers, and that each finger believes it's a totally separate entity from all the other fingers. Upon death, however, we discover that each of those fingers is actually part of the same hand. If we were to realize this while we were alive, we'd refuse to kill anyone; we'd refuse to cut off any of the fingers of our own hand.

As I mentioned earlier, when I was in the NDE state, not only was I without my physical body, but I was also without my gender, my race, my culture, my religion, my beliefs, and my ego. Yet without all these earthly elements, I wasn't a reduced version of myself—I was actually something far, far greater! I was expanded, more powerful, more magnificent. In fact, I realized that earth-life elements I had always thought of as me actually reduced me, limited me, and made me far less than what I actually am. Without these narrow boundaries, I was limitless. I was part of—and one with—everything.

Here in three-dimensional earth-life, however, contrasts and differences are necessary to create what we see as reality. We call this *duality*. We can perceive something only in contrast with something else. Yet by focusing on these differences, we often see each other as enemies.

In this life, we find it almost impossible to be nonjudgmental because we have to discern, discriminate, and judge all the time. That's how we navigate life. We have to be able to perceive good and bad, negative and positive, light and dark—qualities we perceive as being in opposition to each other. And as we constantly judge and compare, we are always making choices. We believe that some choices are better than others when they make us, and those around us, happier. And certainly, some choices *do* seem to serve us better than others. Learning which choices serve us best is how we negotiate life.

What I learned in the NDE state, though, is that those qualities we perceive as opposites are really *not* in opposition. They work in tandem, and if you eliminate one, the other vanishes as well. We can't know one without knowing the other. In that state of total clarity, where everything becomes known simultaneously, there is no division.

This means that not only could I see both sides of the coin at once, and at all times, but also that I understood that they're actually the same unit—the way a Möbius strip really has only one side, even though it appears to have two. In fact, in non-duality, we *become* the coin and thoroughly understand that both sides are necessary for anything to exist at all. After all, it's not possible to have a one-sided coin. So in that realm, I felt nothing but complete acceptance for the way life works. In fact, I felt more than acceptance—I felt total, unconditional love for everyone and everything; I felt compassion and empathy for myself and for all others.

I also understood completely why I do everything I do—and why everyone else does as they do—no matter how bad or how hurtful our acts may seem. Everything became known. The entire illuminated tapestry became clear to me. I understood that many of the things I had done during my life, including any hurtful actions, were done from a perspective of limitation. In other words, I understood that when I had hurt others, those acts came from my own pain, my own fears, my own ignorance, and my own lack of awareness. I had done the best I could with what I knew at any given time. From the perspective of that infinite realm, I understood that we are destructive only as a last resort, hurtful only when we truly believe—rightly or wrongly from our limited perspective—that we have no other choice.

When we die, we will be able to see the whole picture of our life at one glance, understanding why events and circumstances happened the way they did and why we made the choices we made. I believe that's true even for criminals. In many cases, those we label as evil can be seen as victims of their own limited perspective. We only have to observe that there are more men than women in prisons, for example, to see that play out. Why are there more people of certain ethnic groups incarcerated than others? Why are the majority of people in prisons from the lower socio-economic levels? How have we as a society—with our prejudices and roadblocks, our heavy expectations and assumptions—helped create these criminals?

Behind every crime is not only one perpetrator, but a complexity of people and events that all make sense from a cosmic perspective. We seem to think that if we can just get one particular person or group of evildoers behind bars, the world will be a better place. But what we don't realize is that everyone that person encountered in their life and every experience they ever had—whether it was being bullied in school, being discriminated against for their race, or being mistreated by family—is part of what impelled them to make the decisions they made and to act the way they acted.

During my NDE, the realization that we are all connected was so strong that even if I had thought about someone who was a murderer or child abuser—someone whom I hated and felt utter contempt for in physical life—I would have felt nothing but total understanding and compassion for them in that expanded state. In fact, I would have felt empathy for the pain that caused them to choose that path in the first place, and I would have felt complete, unconditional love for both the perpetrator and their victims. My NDE enabled me to understand that people hurt others either out of ignorance or because they are in pain, or because they are so disconnected from their true essence that they don't have the ability to feel emotions (whether that is due to having been abused in some way or because of mental illness).

I have often come under attack on social media for expressing that there is no judgment in the other realm. This view is not popular, especially because it goes against the dogma of traditional religions, and also because we like to think in terms of "us and them," and to believe that those who we feel have wronged us will be justly dealt with in the afterlife. I sometimes find it challenging to share the truth of what I experienced when that truth goes against popular belief, but I have to trust that whoever needs to hear my truth will hear it and benefit from it.

This was confirmed for me some time ago when I received a letter from a man in prison. He wrote that he had been given a 20-year sentence with no parole, so I guessed his crime must have been pretty serious. While still in prison serving time, he had seen Wayne Dyer interview me on his PBS television special. I had specifically said in that interview that there is no judgment on the other side for anything we have ever done here because everything becomes clear and known. From that plane, we understand why we do what we do.

This prisoner was so intrigued by my testimony that he called his sister from the prison and asked her to buy my book and send it to him. After that, he wrote to me, telling me how much relief he had received from watching the interview and reading my book. Society had convinced him that he would go to hell for his crimes, and as a result, he was afraid of death. He knew what he had done was wrong, and although I didn't ask him what it was, he said in his letter that he was young and stupid when he committed the crime. Given another chance or under different circumstances, he knows he would never have done it.

He'd been 20 years old, and his life had been going well up to that point, he explained, and then he'd had a moment of weakness when he was together with his friends. He said he regretted the crime, which he saw as the biggest mistake of his life. He was already paying with his life, he said, and the thought that he would have to continue to pay for this mistake after death, through all of eternity, had haunted him. He wrote that my testimony brought him peace for the first time since he'd been in prison. He was willing to use his life to pay for his mistake, and now he knew that he could die in peace when his time came. His letter brought tears to my eyes. It was what I needed to assure me that I was doing the right thing in sharing my truth instead of pandering to what the general public wanted to hear. I reached out to him to tell him how much his letter had helped me, and he too was moved.

The Grand Tapestry

Because no words in our language can adequately describe exactly what I experienced in the nonphysical realm, I frequently use the metaphor of a tapestry to symbolize how I saw that our lives are woven together with the threads of others' lives. Imagine billions of threads spun from every sort of material imaginable, all sparkling with life. There's a different thread representing each and every person who has ever lived, and they're intricately woven together to create amazing, textured images with complex, colorful patterns. The threads intertwine, weaving up, down, around, and through one another with scintillating beauty and grace. The whole tapestry seems alive—a living creation that is quickened by the interweaving of all the individual threads as they form mountains, oceans, elephants, mangoes, skyscrapers, airplanes, sofas, you, me, and everything else that has ever come into being.

Now imagine if you were to follow one strand of thread as it travels through the tapestry, looping in and out of the weave, over and under, touching some threads here, going over others there, slipping under still others later on. This one strand doesn't touch all the threads directly, but some of the threads that it does touch also touch other threads throughout the woof and warp of the entire fabric. As a whole, all the strands connect to make one beautifully cohesive and cosmic work of art that tells an exquisite, balanced story. No individual thread can be extracted without changing everything. Each thread is indispensable to the overall image and is a vital element of the story. That one thread I asked you to follow is a metaphor for you . . . and your life.

While we are living out our lives here in the physical realm, we cannot see the whole tapestry with all its amazing stories and images or how each thread helps make up the entirety. We are aware only of our present moment—one point in time along the journey of our single strand. From this limited perspective, we do our best with what we know in each moment to weave the story that we want told. We may later regret the story we wove, but we know no better in that moment.

Nevertheless, it's important to remember that no matter how we may view the story from the perspective of our physical world, the entire tapestry is perfect from the vantage point of the nonphysical realm. From that higher perspective, everything is as it should be. It cannot be improved upon! So when I was in that other realm, I did not perceive myself as just a single thread. I had an omniscient view of the whole, and I was able to see and feel and understand the *entire story* woven since *forever*, including how I was connected to all other threads—combining now with this one, now with that one.

After I ran away from the marriage my parents arranged for me many years ago, I felt guilty for bringing shame to my family and my fiancé's family. The practice of arranged marriages was normal and expected in my culture, so when I broke the engagement, many in my community ostracized me. But what if I had actually done nothing "wrong" and instead had gotten it *right*? What if the universe wasn't punishing me or causing me to suffer for some bad karma from a previous life—as I had been led to believe at that time? What if my actions had actually helped highlight—at least within my community—some of the fundamental problems of arranged marriages, particularly for those like myself who grew up in multicultural communities? Maybe I was *meant* to step out in courage for the purpose of helping others, especially parents within my community who had marriageable children, to think twice before making the same error in judgment for their adult children.

We are all connected. What each of us does affects everyone else, the whole tapestry. I no longer carry guilt from running away, nor do I beat myself up for unintentionally hurting others. What I now realize is that maybe that's the way it was meant to unfold in the greater perspective of the universe. I now know to release any feelings of guilt or self-criticism and to trust that everything is as it should be in this exquisite, infinite, cosmic tapestry.

We Are All Connected

So many different synchronicities have taken place in my life over the last few years that confirm for me again and again how connected we actually are. For me, a synchronicity is when a connection is made between myself and someone else that is so utterly beyond chance, so stunningly transparent and unlikely, that the idea of simple coincidence is way too far-fetched even to consider.

For example, when I was deep in a coma in a Hong Kong hospital in February 2006, my husband was by my side, willing me to come back, while at the same time, my mother was at a Hindu temple, praying to Shiva, whom she has strong faith in. Simultaneously, my Buddhist sister-in-law, Mona, was in India, doing a 10-hour deep meditation and chanting for my health that was spread over a period of three days. Mona told me later that within five minutes of completing the 10 hours of deep meditation and chanting, she got a phone call from my family saying that I was out of intensive care and was being moved to a room in the recovery section of the hospital.

Yet another example of synchronicity is how Wayne Dyer came into my life and helped me get my first book published. As I detailed in *Dying to Be Me*, just as I decided I was ready to share my story with a wider audience, author and past-life regressionist Mira Kelley happened to read an account that I wrote about my NDE on the Internet. She was so struck by my experience that the very next day she mentioned my story to Wayne during a phone call, and he wanted to read it, too. She sent it to him, and he was so taken with it that he immediately decided to track me down and help me publish a book about my experience.

Even on a smaller scale, synchronicities keep happening that not only confirm for me our interconnection, but also add spice and joy to my life on a daily basis. People seem to keep willing me to appear—or I will them to appear—and suddenly, there we are together, touching each other's lives in a very profound way.

A few years ago I was in India, visiting my mother in the city of Pune only weeks after my book was released. I had just been on Wayne Dyer's public television special in the U.S., and my life was changing at an accelerated pace. I was craving the feeling of being home in the warm embrace of my mum, so I went to spend some downtime with her and to take a break from the hectic pace of traveling.

Pune is an enormous city of 5.5 million people and has been considered an important spiritual center for most of its nearly

3,000-year history. While my mother lives in a quiet section of the city, one afternoon we were visiting the bustling downtown area with its myriad labyrinthine streets and alleyways, all twisting and turning in a riot of confusion, traffic, noise, mobs of people, and every kind of shop and stall under the sun. As we walked, I took in the anarchy of colors, sounds, scents, and the explosion of humanity colliding in glorious exuberance.

We wove our way between rickshaws, bicycles, and scooters ringing their bells to announce their passage, all the while trying to dodge the bullock carts that plodded along at a snail's pace. We wound down narrow streets lined with vendors selling spicy cooked vegetables, bread, fried snacks, sweets, plastic toys, beautiful fabrics, clothes, colorful handbags and hats, sandals, balloons, kitchen utensils, and more. These sights and sounds mixed with the smells of incense, red curry, both fresh and rotting vegetables, gasoline fumes, perfumes, and cow dung. The entire scene was the kind of feast for the senses that can only be experienced, never fully described.

As I was taking all this in, I caught sight of a gorgeous skirt hanging in the window of a very small, nearly invisible shop nestled between a spice vendor and a tailoring store, right in the middle of all the activity. The colorful skirt, made of a patchwork of beautiful Indian fabrics, called to me like a siren's song, beckoning me in a way I couldn't resist, so my mother and I entered the little shop to take a closer look.

"Hi!" I called out. "Can I take a look at the colorful skirt displayed in the window?"

"Of course you may," said a pretty young woman with a lovely smile who came out from behind the counter. She went toward the front of the shop to pull the skirt down from the display window and handed it to me.

"Try it on so you can see how it drapes on you," she suggested in a friendly manner as I faced a full-length mirror, holding the skirt at my waist. "I really think it will suit you."

Her manner was not at all pushy, just very genuine and caring. I could tell this was her own shop and she took pride in her offerings. She wasn't just concerned about making a sale; she was also concerned with honoring and respecting our human connection.

"Do you have a fitting room?" I asked.

"Yes, back here in this corner," she said. "There's a curtain that we will draw around you. Just stand behind the curtain and you can try the skirt on."

I went behind the curtain and tried on the skirt. When I came out, both the shop owner and my mother said it was a very lovely skirt that really suited me. As I turned to go back behind the curtain to change, the young woman asked, "Where are you from? Your accent is not local, so I know you're not from around here."

"Yes, you're right," I answered from behind the curtain. "I don't live in India. I live in Hong Kong. I grew up there."

"Wow, that's an amazing coincidence!" she exclaimed as I handed her the skirt with the intention of purchasing it. "I'm just now in the middle of reading this astounding book written by an Indian woman who also happens to have grown up in Hong Kong. Her name is Anita Moorjani. Have you heard of her?"

My jaw dropped when she said my name!

"That's *me*! You're reading my book!" I said in total surprise. Then it was her jaw that dropped.

"What? You're kidding me! No way! I don't believe it!" she cried out, visibly shocked. She reached behind the counter and pulled out my book with its familiar blue cover, turned to the back where my photo was, and said, "Oh my god! It really *is* you!" Then she ran outside the store and called for all the vendors from the neighboring stalls and shops to come in.

"You know that book I've been glued to this past week? The one I've been reading during my lunch hour every day while telling everyone not to interrupt me?" she asked. "This is the author of that book! She has come into my shop!" she said emphatically, bursting with pride as I smiled from ear to ear. Then she told someone to bring some spicy chai for both my mother and me as she pulled out some wooden folding stools from behind the counter and placed them in the center of the little shop.

"Please, sit down! I can't let you leave my shop so soon!" she said. "I can't believe you are here, *in my store*!"

I was tongue-tied. I didn't know what to say. This was such an astonishing confluence of connections in one of the most unlikely places on the planet that I could only marvel at it. My book had barely been out two months, and to find it here, in Pune, being read by the shopkeeper of a tiny boutique in a crowded warren of streets in the absolute middle of a muddled megalopolis, was almost too much to take in.

"My name is Gita, by the way," she said, still looking as astonished as I felt.

"How did you come to be reading my book?" I asked, knowing that it was not yet available in India, since it had only just come out in the U.S. and a handful of other countries.

"My cousin lives in the U.K.," Gita explained, "and she read it first. Then she sent it to me saying I had to read it, too."

"It's incredible how small the world has become, and how we are all connected," I said. "It's amazing how your cousin, far off in the U.K., sends you my book—and then I bump into you like this!"

"As I was reading the book, I was wishing and wishing I could meet you some day," Gita told me. "I had so many things going on in my head that I wanted to say to you. It was as though I was willing you to show up, and here you are!" Her eyes brimmed with tears as she spoke.

"You have indeed willed me to be here," I said, certain that I was meant to be there for her, and that she was meant to touch my life in some way, as well. "I feel I am here because of you, so please ask me any questions you have."

Her eyes still filled with tears, Gita told me about her son who was autistic. I could tell she was a beautiful and loving mother to her son, and he was blessed to have her as his mother. Yet she was now dealing with some challenging issues, and she felt as though she and her son didn't understand each other very well anymore. She found the situation heartbreaking, and she asked if I had any advice.

"Communicate with your heart and not with your words," I told her. "Remember that we are all connected. So in this respect, if *you* feel good, your son will also feel good. So it's really important to look after yourself and your needs.

"As it is, children are very sensitive to this connection we all have, but I've noticed that children with special needs or challenges are often even more sensitive to those around them," I continued. "Your son feels whatever you feel. So start by asking yourself what you need to feel more fulfilled and how you can love and support yourself more. I am certain that when you start to feel happy again, it will have an impact on your son."

Gita looked visibly relieved, and then the conversation lightened and we talked about synchronicities and how amazing our meeting each other was—in a teeming city of 5.5 million people that's on the opposite side of the planet from where I lived! We sat and chatted for about an hour, and then I had to leave. As I was about to pay for the skirt, Gita pushed the parcel into my hands and said, "Take it. It's a gift from me."

"I couldn't!" I responded.

"No, I insist," she said. "I want you to remember this chance meeting whenever you wear it."

I was so touched, so moved by her generous spirit. I accepted Gita's gift with great love and we hugged like parting sisters.

"Come back again," she called out.

"I will," I replied. "The very next time I'm in Pune."

My mother and I left the store with a light and buoyant step, knowing that the intricate workings of the universe would always delight and uplift us, showing us the way wherever we went.

Intend Only Love

Each night before I go to sleep, as I lie in bed reviewing my day, I send love to every single person on the planet, no matter who they are. After all, we are all connected. It doesn't matter to me what they have done, whom they have helped, or whom they have hurt—even if it's me who they've harmed. Some are undoubtedly serial killers, murderers, and rapists. I deliberately intend love for *everyone* by visualizing myself expanding and reaching out and hugging every single person, including those on death row. Maybe if they had known what it was like to feel love, they would not have killed in the first place. The antidote to hatred and violence is never more hatred and violence. The antidote is love.

Living Heaven *Here and Now*

If "Coincidences are just coincidences" is a *myth*, then what could be the *truth*?

Consider These Possible Truths

- We are part of one big, cosmic whole, intricately connected in ways we can't see and can't even imagine in the physical realm.

- If we *are* all connected, then whatever harms another also harms us, and whatever helps another also helps us.

- If we could see this physical world from that connected state of non-duality, we would see that everything that happens is perfect just as it is, even if it doesn't seem that way from our more limited earthly perspective.

Tips and Exercises

- When you beat yourself up and judge your past actions as wrong, remind yourself that you did the best you could do at the time, considering what you then knew or felt.

- Learn to follow your hunches when you feel guided to go somewhere or do or say something. Stay open to the possibility of making synchronistic connections with others.

- Practice becoming more compassionate with someone you judge only slightly; as you become comfortable opening your heart and being more accepting of that person or their actions, extend your compassion to someone else who you have judged more harshly than the first person. Each time you become comfortable extending compassion at one level, work toward the next—and keep going.

- Spend as much or more time reading or listening to uplifting stories about others as you spend paying attention to news about negative events. Remember that even when everything seems gloom and doom, that's just what the media is reporting. An equal amount of good also exists in the world—so without denying the bad, be on the lookout for the good and appreciate it as fully as possible.

- When visiting another country or spending time with people of a different culture, look for what you have in common—such as a love for children or devotion to family. Learn to see things as being *different* rather than labeling them as being *strange*. Teach your children to do the same from as early an age as possible.

Questions to Ask Yourself

- How might I be holding myself back or even hurting myself by looking at people and situations from a limited, judgmental perspective?

- What conditions or circumstances might drive someone to do or say something that would hurt another?

- If I knew for sure that I was connected to everyone and everything, how might that effect what I think, what I say, and what I do?

- What feelings of guilt am I still holding on to? Can I take a giant step back and see what I said or did from a different, more compassionate perspective? If not, am I able to have that perspective for the actions of a dear friend or loved one? What would it take to give myself the same amount of understanding and compassion that I give others?

I know when I am experiencing true oneness when . . .

- Delightful synchronicities unfold, reminding me that what may seem random and coincidental is really part of a much larger plan I am being guided to follow.

- I am quick to give myself and others the benefit of the doubt, realizing that everything ultimately works together for good.

- My initial reaction to a hurtful situation is to show at least some degree of compassion for those who have caused the pain or chaos instead of reacting with judgment or anger.

MYTH:
WE PAY FOR OUR
SINS AT DEATH

A s our flight circled above Los Angeles, preparing for landing, I gazed out the window at the rooftops below. I could see parks, gardens, swimming pools, and cars stuck in traffic. From the air, they all looked like little toys.

When we fly, I always take the window seat and Danny always takes the aisle. He likes having the flexibility to get up and walk around to stretch his legs, while I love looking out the window and getting a feel for the city where we're about to land. Seeing the buildings and the neighborhoods, the highways and the suspension bridges, the mountains and the farmland all excites me. I even love looking out the window when we are above the clouds because it gives me a feeling of merging with the universe, much like how it felt when I had the NDE in 2006.

"Look, Danny! There's the famous Hollywood sign!" I said excitedly, moving my head out of the way so he could see. This was not our first time landing at LAX. In fact, most of our domestic flights in the U.S. seemed to connect through this airport, and we were starting to become very familiar with it as I was doing more and more speaking engagements in and around California.

As Danny leaned over my shoulder to look out the window, we felt a sudden upward jolt, and the aircraft immediately started to ascend toward the clear, blue sky.

"Ladies and gentlemen, this is your captain speaking," a male voice announced over the public address system. "I do apologize, but we have had to abort our landing. We are having a minor mechanical problem with the landing gear. We are working to resolve it now and will be attempting to land again in a few minutes. Do not be alarmed when you see fire trucks and ambulances surrounding the aircraft on the tarmac when we land. This is purely a safety procedure."

Danny and I looked at each other with an expression of bemusement. "Well, at least we're together," I said. "If we go this time, you won't have to come and bring me back!" We were joking, but nine years earlier, when I was on what everyone presumed was my deathbed, no one was doing much joking. On February 2, 2006, I was in a coma with end-stage lymphoma, and my organs were shutting down. I had struggled with this cancer for four long years, and on that February day, the doctors told my family that I was in my final hours.

During that challenge, Danny had been my strength. He'd kept me going, and when I was finally in the coma, he never left my side, holding my hand and whispering to me, willing me to come back. During my sojourn on the other side, I'd felt that Danny's life purpose and mine were linked and that if I had chosen to die at that time, he would soon have followed, since he would not then have been able to complete his purpose. Yet it didn't feel as if that would've been a bad thing. It just felt like we were meant to be together, in life and in death, and so if I chose death I still wouldn't lose him.

We are opposites in so many ways—Danny likes cold weather, while I like warmth; he likes the rain, and I like the sunshine; he likes the city, yet I like the seaside; I'm more artistic, he's more analytical; I'm more visual, he's more technical. Yet we always seem to be so in sync, our lives so intertwined, that it's often hard to determine where he ends and I begin.

"We are not going to die," Danny responded in a droll tone as the airplane climbed above Los Angeles. But he reached for my hand and held it as he said, "If the landing gear doesn't come down, they will do a belly landing."

"Oh great," I said with a sigh. "Isn't that where they keep the luggage? All I need is for the belly of the plane to rip open and for all my clothes, shawls, shoes, and purses to be strewn all over the tarmac!"

"No, that wouldn't happen because that's not how they do it!" Danny said, after letting out a chuckle. "They spray foam all the way down the runway, and that acts as a lubricant and fire retardant." Although he knew I was only making light of the situation, his analytical mind had worked through the scenario and come up with a resolution to the problem even before it had occurred—which is so like him. And that's something that I have really grown to depend on.

Our conversation was suddenly interrupted by the grating sound of the landing gear descending. The relief of the passengers was palpable as the flight finally made its touchdown on the tarmac in front of Los Angeles's Tom Bradley International Terminal.

A Dark Stranger

As we made our way to gate 44 to board our connecting flight to San Jose, I thought I noticed a man staring at me. But when I looked back at him, he looked away, so I dismissed it as my imagination.

At the appointed gate, Danny and I showed the gate agent our boarding passes, only to be told that the flight was going to be delayed by two hours due to foggy conditions! Wow—a two-hour delay just to take a one-hour flight! The gate agent was empathetic, but there was nothing she could do. We asked if we could switch to another flight, but when she checked for us, she came up empty. We were in good company, though, since the city had experienced a whole morning of fog. All the flights that day were behind schedule.

All we could do was settle down and get comfortable, so Danny and I found some seats, and he started looking around for a wall socket where he could charge his iPad. We were going to have a long wait. I wanted to grab a cup of tea before pulling out my own iPad to check my e-mail, so I put my carry-on down on the seat and asked Danny if he'd like anything from the café. He asked me to get him a cup of coffee.

I made my way to the café across the hallway, the only one in this particular segment of the terminal, and ordered a spicy chai for me and a coffee for Danny. As I walked back toward our seats, from the corner of my eye I once again became aware of someone looking at me. When I turned to look, I saw the same gentleman I'd noticed before. But this time, he didn't turn away. His dark, piercing eyes looked straight at me, and he gave me a slight smile and a nod, as if to acknowledge that he knew who I was. He appeared to be in his mid- to late 40s, with graying hair that I guessed used to be quite dark. But what stood out the most for me was a certain sadness about his expression.

I nodded and smiled, then made my way back to our seats with the tea and coffee. I set the drinks on the ground just in front of our seats and sat down. I reached into my bag and pulled out my iPad, and when I looked up, the man with the sad, dark eyes was standing right in front of me, looking a little self-conscious.

"Hi," he said. "Are you Anita Moorjani?"

"Yes, I am," I answered, surprised he would know my name.

"I've read your book and watched many of your videos on YouTube," he said with a hint of a smile. "I've received a lot of comfort from your message."

"Thank you! I'm so happy to hear that my message has been helpful to you!" I said as a broad smile spread across my face. It still takes me by surprise when people recognize me at random places in public, even though it happens more and more.

"Um . . . can I talk to you about something for a minute?" he asked. He obviously knew I wasn't rushing to catch a flight since I had just purchased a cup of tea and had settled into my seat with my iPad.

"Sure! Why don't you sit down?" I responded warmly, gesturing toward the empty seat next to me.

"My name is Ron, by the way," he said, holding out his hand to shake mine as he sat down.

"Nice to meet you, Ron. And this is my husband, Danny," I replied, gesturing toward Danny, who was sitting on my other side.

"Hi, Danny! I'm so sorry to be taking up your wife's attention."

"Don't worry about it, Ron. I'm getting used to it," Danny responded lightheartedly.

"I can't believe the synchronicity of running into you like this. I have your book, *Dying to Be Me*, right here." He pulled out a copy of the book. It looked well thumbed, the pages dog-eared.

"I read it many times months ago, but I carried it on this flight to reread it," he explained. "And as I was reading it, I was thinking of all the questions I would ask you if I were ever to meet you. And now here you are! I still can't believe it!" he said incredulously.

Although this sort of thing happens to me more and more frequently—where people will me into their lives, and then I show up—I still found myself shuffling my feet and blushing, at a loss for words. Danny came to my rescue.

"Welcome to our world, Ron! Ever since Anita's brush with death, our life has been so full of synchronicities that we don't even question them anymore. I wake up every morning and ask her, 'So what are you going to manifest *today*?' Then I fasten my seatbelt and prepare for another day of adventure and surprise!"

Ron laughed and looked immediately at ease.

"Well, I do believe there are no accidents in this life," he replied, "and that everything has a greater purpose, often beyond what we can see. So my meeting you here just seems to be part of that expanded, infinite consciousness you write about so eloquently in your book."

"Please feel free to ask whatever questions you may have," I said with a smile, "but don't be surprised if you find yourself in the pages of my next book!" Ron gave an initial laugh; then he looked at the floor, beginning to struggle a bit with his emotions.

Living with Guilt

"My wife, Trish, passed away six months ago," he started off, "and I'm having a lot of trouble coming to terms with that. I still miss her so much! I don't know if I'll ever get over losing her."

"I'm so sorry to hear that!" I said with genuine sadness for what he was going through. "There's no time limit for grief. Give yourself all the time you need, and don't judge yourself if you aren't ready to start living life again."

It has always surprised me how much emphasis most spiritual and religious teachings place on getting the rituals just right for the one who has passed, yet they offer so little in the way of grief support for those who are left behind—those who must somehow cope with the loss, the pain, and the gaping void that remains when their loved one leaves this plane for the next.

"Take care of yourself right now. This is your number one job. Trish would want you to do that," I said, hoping it would help. But I sensed that there was something more to the story that he hadn't yet shared, some deeper issue that was troubling him. As if on cue, Ron looked down at the floor again.

"What makes it worse," he said slowly, "is that she took her own life. She committed suicide, and I've been feeling really guilty about it."

And there it was.

"That's when someone gave me your book," he continued, meeting my gaze again. "At first, I was really scared to read it. I was frightened about what I might find out. I was completely wracked with guilt—Trish overdosed on a bottle of pills one night while I was away on a business trip. I felt awful that I didn't see it coming and that I couldn't stop her! I haven't been able to sleep since that night."

My heart went out to Ron. I was now feeling the guilt and sadness he carried in his heavy heart, and I wished that I could just reach inside and remove the emotions that were weighing him down so heavily. Grief is difficult enough to deal with, but guilt adds a whole other layer that complicates the entire grieving process.

"One day, someone sent me an e-mail with a video link," Ron continued, "and it was one of your videos. So since someone had given me your book and someone else had sent me a link to your video, I took that as a sign that I was meant to listen to your message. I started by watching your video, and it brought me great comfort to know that my wife is probably okay instead of being judged for choosing to check out like that. That was also one of my great fears—that she might be punished!

"After listening to the video, I read your book—and I loved it! The book brought me even more comfort, and I was so grateful. After that, I started listening to all your interviews on the Internet. I just started Googling you and devouring everything you said. But even though I've been feeling a little better since hearing your message, I still have a lot of questions. And I really don't know how to deal with the guilt."

His eyes started to well up with tears, so I reached for my handbag, pulled out a tissue, and held it out to him as I said, "Wow, this has really been a difficult time for you. I'm so sorry to hear about this." He took the tissue and turned away, discreetly wiping away the tears before they could roll down his cheeks.

Dead Isn't Dead

In that moment, although I felt terrible for Ron, watching what he was going through made me feel so grateful for having Danny in my life. Even though I've tasted the bliss of death and know it to be a perfect and wonderful state, the thought of living in this world without Danny was not a thought I cared to entertain. So I knew that at this moment, assuring Ron that his wife had gone on to a better place was not going to be enough. It was not going to alleviate his grief and guilt.

I know from my experience speaking with others who've lost loved ones that death cracks us open completely. It changes our world, our purpose, and our focus so dramatically that we can find it hard to imagine a future without our loved one in it. For many whose entire purpose revolved around a loved one who is now gone, life as they knew it no longer exists. So I knew that giving him some clever self-help quote was not going to cut it right then. I could sense that Ron needed something more—something to keep him going. Yet I wanted to be careful not to sound glib.

"She does not want you to feel guilty for what she did," I told Ron.

"Really? Are you sure?" he said as his eyes widened with hope.

"Yes, I'm sure," I said. "When I was without my body, all I felt was total unconditional love for everyone in my family. I didn't want them to suffer because of me at all! I wanted them to be happy, and nothing would've made me more joyful than to see them happy. I can assure you that that's what Trish wants for you right now. She wants to see you happy. That's what all our deceased loved ones want for us. If Trish would want you to know anything right now, it would be that what she did is not your fault. She did it out of her own pain and her own inability to deal with that pain. Of that I am sure!"

I saw a hint of relief break across Ron's face, and then it disappeared almost as quickly as he added, "But we had an argument just before she took her life. I feel so awful about it! My mind is going through every 'what if' scenario. What if we hadn't had an argument? What if I'd told her I loved her instead? Would she not have done what she did?" Then his gaze returned to the floor. "And even if she *is* in a great place," he said softly, "I didn't get a last chance to tell her that I loved her."

"You can talk to her now," I insisted. "She can hear you, I promise. You can resolve anything that wasn't finished. Just talk to her as though she is there. She actually already knows what's in your heart and mind, but it will help you to talk to her directly. Go into a quiet space, and she will hear you. I could hear all my husband's thoughts when I was no longer in my body. I knew everything he was thinking, and I knew how much he loved me. All I felt for him was unconditional love. I know Trish must now feel the same for you. If she could communicate with you right now, I'm sure she would want you to know this."

I paused a moment before adding, "I don't believe anyone really goes before their time. I don't think you had anything to do with her leaving. People don't take their life because of one argument. It's much more complex than that, with many different elements coming into play. Even if you hadn't had the argument, or even if you had told her you loved her that day, sooner or later, something else would have triggered her desire to take her own life. It has more to do with the way the person interprets their life's experiences—the filter through which they view the world and their place in it, and that's something beyond your control.

"From where she is now, she would want you to find peace and happiness," I continued. "She loves you unconditionally, and nothing will make her happier than to see you happy again."

Judgment Day Cometh Not

Ron's expression seemed to lighten up considerably, but then he asked, "What about judgment? I grew up believing that taking your own life leads to some pretty serious consequences—and although I've heard you say many times in interviews that that's not the case, I sometimes still feel scared for her. How can you be so sure that she's not being judged?" As he asked that question, the sad and worried look returned.

"There's definitely no judgment at all, and especially not for suicide!" I assured him. "Some people may have at some point what they call a 'life review' where they evaluate their own life, but in the end all that remains is unconditional love. A person has to be in a lot of pain to choose to leave this life—they're not going to get more punishment than that in the next! There's only unconditional love and compassion for her where she is. Trust me—I know this!"

"That's reassuring," Ron responded, "but I've heard of some people who've had a negative near-death experience—they experienced darkness or something really fearful in their brief time in the other realm. Sometimes I worry about Trish, and I hope she's not going through something like that as a repercussion for what she did. I think that's what worries me the most!"

"I know that for those who may have had such a negative experience, it was very real for them," I said. "And I certainly don't want to discount anyone else's experience. But I truly want to assure you that everyone finally makes it to a positive place! Experts who do research into NDE phenomena have stressed that very few people have truly negative experiences. Often, those people are still playing out the fears accumulated from this life. You know how fear-filled life can be! Many of us are brought up on a constant diet of fear that plagues our minds, and sometimes with a sudden death we carry those fears with us to the other side. If we hang around in that realm long enough, though, those fears dissolve because we lose our attachment to our mind, and then we are reconnected with our true essence—unconditional love. In that state, all we feel is compassion, fearlessness, and total acceptance."

When I touched on that, Ron's expression grew serious. "Trish was very fearful of death and of what would happen afterward," he shared. "She had a very difficult and abusive childhood that really messed her up. As a result, she did some things she shouldn't have done. Her upbringing instilled strong religious beliefs in her about hell and being punished for sins. Because of this, she often felt God was going to punish her when she died. I hope she's not going through a personal hell because of her beliefs."

Death, Fear, and Religion

Since my own near-death experience, I often marvel at how inventive we humans are and at all the stories we've created over the millennia to explain what happens to us after death. Like Trish, I was also extremely fearful of death before my NDE. I was afraid of karma, and in fact I believed that my cancer was *caused* by karma, so I spent my life doing things to ensure a positive karma after death. But often those positive actions stemmed not so much from love, empathy, and compassion, but more from a fear of negative karma.

During my NDE, I was not only without my physical body, but I was also without my race, my culture, my gender, and my religion! I had shed all those layers of values and beliefs that my physical self had accumulated over this lifetime. I was surprised to find that all of those pieces of my physical-life identity had nothing to do with my *infinite* self! So if my infinite self didn't include those elements, then what was left after stripping away all those layers? It wasn't a reduced element of myself, but in fact, something far, far greater. I was pure essence . . . pure consciousness . . . pure love . . . pure God. Label it what you will, but no words could ever match the totality of what I felt. I experienced nothing but love, empathy, and compassion for myself and for everyone who had ever come into my life, whether they had seemingly hurt me or helped me. I realized that even those who had seemingly hurt me had somehow moved me to the next level of my life in a positive way, even if it didn't feel like that at the time.

I could call that process my "life review," but that hardly begins to describe the ecstatic experience. I felt no pain, no anger, no judgment (toward myself or others), and no guilt—I just felt so loved and so safe.

After coming back into this life and into my body, I remember wondering why we were never taught about how unconditionally loved we are, how pure we are, and how amazing and powerful and magnificent we are. Why are we never taught that there's no judgment, or that the most important thing we can focus on is love, not fear of retribution? But then, who would tell us this? Most of us—even those who teach others about what happens after death—don't really know this information. All we know is what our culture or religious tenets teach, tenets written thousands of years ago by men in a completely different culture and era.

Believing we will be judged in the afterlife really alters the way we live life here—and often not in a positive way. This belief keeps us in fear of what will happen to us on the other side, so instead of doing good for the sake of love and goodness itself, we can easily find ourselves acting out of fear of being punished after we die. And fear is *not* love.

During my NDE, any regrets for what I'd done wrong were my own and didn't come from any entity outside myself. I experienced no judgmental being who was separate from me, who had been watching me, waiting for me to screw up and ready to punish me when I did. Society conditions us into thinking that we are being watched and judged, and that judgment comes from outside ourselves, because we live in a world of duality. But in nonduality, there's only pure consciousness, pure unconditional love, and total acceptance. There's nothing outside of us. Everything's connected; everything becomes known. And we realize that both the victim and the perpetrator are part of the *same consciousness*. There is no "us and them"—it's *all* us. We are all two sides of the same coin.

I wish I had known this earlier. I wish I had not been taught to fear the afterlife because I was somehow going to be judged and punished. I wish that I had instead been taught empathy and compassion for myself and for the other members of our earth family, as well as how we are all connected and how we all affect each other.

We Are Guided

Sitting in the Los Angeles airport, I tried to convey this all to Ron.

"I know without a doubt that Trish is fine. Truly she is!" I assured him. "So much so that I think our meeting was in some way guided by her. Bringing me into your path may be her way to assure you that she's okay and wants you to find peace in your life again. You just need to do whatever you can to take care of yourself. *She's* fine, but she is still concerned about *your* well-being."

"Thank you! I really needed to hear that," Ron said with great relief. His posture visibly changed, and I could tell he had truly taken our conversation to heart.

"I'm glad that's helpful," I said. "And I'm also certain that she continues to watch over you. Our loved ones really do keep an eye on us. And as I said before, Trish can hear you if you talk to her, so it's not too late to have a conversation with her. You can talk to her as though she's physically here—saying whatever you didn't get the chance to say when she was still alive. I'm sure it'll be very cathartic for you, and I very much encourage it. In fact, have as many conversations as you need to have but perhaps when you are alone, so people don't think you're nuts!" I said, trying to inject a bit of humor.

"People already think I'm nuts, so that's not an issue!" Ron replied with a laugh.

"Welcome to the club!" I said, and then we both started laughing.

"By the way, I'm pretty sure Trish will try to communicate with you," I added. "She will want you to know she's fine. During the quietest times, you may start to sense her presence, intuiting things that she wants you to know."

"I've actually started to feel her presence from time to time," Ron said a little excitedly. "In fact, it was after listening to one of your video interviews that I started feeling better, and then I was able to relax a little bit. Ever since then, I've been feeling sort of guided by her. I even felt as though she was the one who guided me to your videos, as though she knew I'd feel better after listening to you speak."

I felt myself blushing ever so slightly.

"I'm so glad I was the catalyst for your wife helping you!" I said with genuine gratitude.

At that moment, as if on cue, the gate agents started making announcements for our flight to San Jose. Danny turned to us and said, "Sorry to interrupt, but we need to board now."

I could sense Ron's lightness, in stark contrast to the heavy-hearted man I had bumped into earlier, and I knew his newfound joy came not only from my words, but also from the knowledge that his wife was still with him, guiding him—and that in fact, she was probably the one who led him to me that day, so that he could know that she really *was* fine!

As we stood up, Ron looked at me and said, "I don't know how to thank you!"

"You already have," I said with a mischievous smile. "You've given me another chapter for my next book!"

"Please use anything that you feel will help others," he said sincerely. "You have my blessings to use this story."

We hugged, and I noticed his eyes welling up with tears again, as though he knew his wife was present. Danny and I started walking toward the gate, and I gave Ron a final wave before disappearing around the corner and onto the Jetway.

It bothers me that so many of us have been conditioned to expect and fear judgment after death. And the very institutions we go to for answers, solace, and when we are afraid are the ones that perpetuate this erroneous belief! It's as if those institutions are counting on fear to keep us in check and ensure that we won't hurt others. But from what I've noticed about the condition of our planet and the burgeoning prisons we've created, this theory doesn't seem to be working.

I believe that knowing the truth that we *are* love and that we're loved unconditionally—together with the knowledge that we're all connected—can help us feel true empathy and compassion for one another. If we all took that knowledge into our hearts, we'd act with more kindness and reverence for ourselves, each other, and even our planet. And our approach to life, as well as our approach to death, would be one of love, not fear. This is my dearest hope.

Living Heaven *Here and Now*

If "At death we are judged and punished for our sins" is a *myth*, then what could be the *truth*?

Consider These Possible Truths

- In the other realm, only unconditional love and compassion for each of us exists, with no judgment or punishment for what we did or didn't do on earth. (This includes those who have committed what are considered in the world of duality to be egregious acts, including suicide or even murder.)

- Our infinite selves—who we are on the other side—are completely devoid of any part of our physical-world identity (such as our race, gender, culture, or religion). We do not take those elements with us, nor would we want to!

- When we are in the other realm, we feel no pain, anger, guilt, fear, or judgment. We feel only total understanding, complete acceptance, unconditional love, and the joyous ecstasy of union with the divine nature of all that is.

Tips and Exercises

- Ask and watch for signs from your loved ones that they are indeed still alive and happy in the other realm and that they want you to know they still love and care for you very much. Signs are as varied as the souls who send them, but they could include the unexpected appearance or unusual behavior of an animal, a light turning on without anyone touching it, or interesting cloud formations that remind you in some way of the person who has passed. Your loved ones may also appear to you in your dreams. The more open and watchful you are, the more likely you'll recognize such a sign.

- Develop a deeper compassion for yourself and others by acknowledging that everyone does the best they can at any given moment with what resources are available to them.

- Realize that what you are most apt to judge in others—and what they are most apt to judge in you—has more to do with the unhealed parts of the person doing the judging than the person being judged. In the other realm, there is nothing to judge—we are simultaneously both sides of the same coin.

- Notice that the most effective parenting does not involve punishing a child for wrongdoing, but rather celebrating the positive. Reflect on why this is so and on whether a similar philosophy may also be at work on a universal scale.

Questions to Ask Yourself

- Do I appease myself with visions of those who have wronged me "getting what's coming to them" once they die? Might I be willing to give up such fantasies and instead begin to embrace the fact that we are all connected and that we are all one—so any ill I wish toward others I am actually wishing toward myself?

- Can I accept that when I judge myself as lacking in some way, I am actually doubting the perfection of the universe?

- If I were on my deathbed right now, what would I want to tell those I was leaving behind on the physical plane? What pieces of myself would I want to share with them? What could I say to them that would make it easier to endure my physical absence?

I know I am not fearful of my own death or the death of my loved ones when. . .

- I know death is not the end, and I will be able to see and even communicate with my loved ones at some point once they pass on—as well as with those I leave behind once I myself leave the earthly realm.

- I am genuinely happy for those who have gone to the other realm, knowing that they are in a state of pure joy, peace, and unconditional love and that they wish the same for me, no matter what our relationship was like on the physical plane.

- I have empathy and compassion for myself and others instead of judgment, and I understand that we are all connected and that we are all expressions of divine love, regardless of what we have said or done on the physical plane.

MYTH:
SPIRITUAL PEOPLE
DON'T HAVE EGOS

"I don't get it," Jane said. "Most spiritual teachings tell us that the ego impedes our spiritual growth and that we need to learn to overcome or transcend it. You are the only one who says to embrace the ego! How do you explain that?"

Jane, a woman attending a retreat I was conducting in the beautiful English countryside, didn't mean any disrespect in asking this question, nor was she trying to be confrontational. She was simply expressing a genuine desire to understand my perspective.

"That's a *great* question," I responded. "Many people ask me this, and there are a *lot* of conflicting opinions about the meaning of the word *ego*, so I understand your confusion. I'm really glad you brought this up!"

About 25 of us were gathered around a fireplace in the cozy restaurant of a little hotel on Burgh Island, a small tidal island off the south coast of Devon County in England. I had been conducting a five-day retreat at Schumacher College, a center for transformative learning, sustainable living, and holistic education located in the nearby village of Dartington. Earlier in the day, our group had taken a trip to the Devon coast, traveling by bus from the college to the village of Bigbury-on-Sea. There, we'd strolled along a beautiful sandy beach and soon found ourselves walking across a causeway to Burgh Island, just off the coast. We'd hiked around, taking in the lovely natural surroundings for about an hour, but then the tide had come in and submerged the path back to the mainland, leaving us stranded.

Although the water wasn't deep, it was freezing cold, so none of us wanted to wade back to the mainland. We'd opted instead to go into the Burgh Island Hotel, a quant old place built in 1929, and wait it out there until the hotel ran its sea tractor—a motor vehicle designed to travel through shallow seawater, carrying passengers on a platform. The hotel manager had explained that we could catch the tractor at about 6 P.M., which was another two hours away. We'd gathered as close to the fireplace as possible, while the manager brought us huge pots of steaming tea and trays of cups. We were sitting comfortably sipping our tea when Jane had asked her question, presenting us with the perfect topic to while away the time.

To Ego . . . or Not to Ego

"So, Jane, in order to respond to your question more accurately, let's try to understand what the word *ego* means to you—or to anyone else here, for that matter," I said, throwing the topic open to the group. "I'm particularly keen to understand what you mean when you say 'the ego impedes our spiritual growth.'"

"I have learned over the years, from all sorts of spiritual teachings, that the purpose of spirituality is to overcome or transcend the ego," Jane began. "My understanding is that the ego is the part of us that is afraid to love and needs to be better than everyone else. A large ego produces an inflated sense of self-worth, encouraging us to be in denial about our faults and become defensive when anyone tries to point them out. In other words, the ego tells us that everything that is wrong is everyone else's fault, never our own. On the other hand, if we were to overcome our ego, then we would be less self-absorbed and far more focused on others, making us much more compassionate and empathic."

Then Kathy chimed in: "I was always told to keep my ego in check because if I didn't, I would be 'full of myself.' Having an inflated ego meant having a really high opinion of myself, and that's considered a bad thing."

"Thanks to both of you for your explanations," I responded. "What you described used to be the way I saw it as well! But my understanding changed when I had the NDE. When I was in the other realm, I realized that every part of my self in this physical life—including my emotions, my mind, and my ego—was necessary to survive and prosper here. The ego gives us our sense of identity, our individuality. It's what allows us to know who we are as individuals and to express our uniqueness. If our ego *weren't* necessary, we wouldn't have been born with it.

"Even though we're all connected, all one, we'd find it very difficult to function in this physical world if we didn't have our egos to give us some sense of where I end and where you begin. We need the ego to be able to discern—just as we learn to tell the difference between green and blue or between vanilla and chocolate. In fact, were it not for our ability to discriminate—to differentiate through comparison and contrast—nothing would exist in this world."

"But doesn't identifying too strongly with the ego cause us to have an overinflated image of ourselves?" asked Brenda. I smiled because this was the point where so many people get stuck—and indeed the point where I, too, had been stuck before my NDE. I knew what I was about to say had the potential to change their perspective 180 degrees.

The Ego Is Our Best Friend

"What if these statements were not true, and our belief in them prevented us from getting to know who we are and from loving ourselves?" I countered. "What is wrong with having a high opinion of ourselves—as well as a high opinion of everyone else? One doesn't preclude the other. In fact, having very low self-esteem makes having relationships with others very challenging!"

"I think I understand why I have so much trouble loving myself!" Sally said suddenly. "It's because I've been conditioned to believe that it's egotistical to love myself, and my notion of being egotistical has been a negative one! I'm afraid of being judged as being egotistical if I love myself!"

"Yes!" I said excitedly. I knew we were on to something important!

"What if the ego is actually not the enemy? What if it's the *belief* that the ego is to be avoided and suppressed that is actually the culprit? I've found that believing the ego has to be denied at all costs has the opposite effect. I end up being obsessed with my ego because I'm constantly focusing on it, denying it, stifling it, containing it, holding it back, and keeping it in check. This causes me to constrain myself in all sorts of ways and inhibits me from expressing the truth of who I am.

"However, the more I love myself and embrace my ego, real-izing it's a necessary part of being here in the physical world, the easier it becomes for me to see myself beyond my ego and to become aware of my infinite self—the self that includes my ego yet transcends it at the same time," I continued. "What if the more I love myself, the less need I have to inflate my ego through self-aggrandizement, bragging, or being boastful? And what if truly loving myself meant that I wouldn't feel the need to be defensive and protective of my ego—so the less I'd need others to love me or to act in a certain way to gratify or massage my ego? I've dis-covered this to be the case in my own life. The more I love myself, the less I associate myself only with my ego because I know that I am something far greater and that I exist with or without my ego."

"You're saying that the ego allows us to know who we are, separate from others?" Henry asked. "I'm trying to reconcile the seeming contradiction of us needing to become aware that we are actually one with all others, while at the same time, being born with an ego that clearly facilitates separation. Why is it so compli-cated? Shouldn't we either be one or be separate? Why do we have to juggle both?"

We Are One . . . and Many

"For the most part," I said, "we *don't* have to juggle both while we're here in the physical world. Most of us rarely, if ever, have any sense of our connection to the 'all-that-is.' We see ourselves as separate and distinct. When I was in the other realm, I was in a state I call 'non-duality.' This means there was no separation—only oneness. There, we are all pure love, pure consciousness, and we are all of the same substance. I was totally in sync with everyone and everything in that state. I had complete empathy—I didn't know where I ended and others began.

"At the same time, I was aware of myself as a unique being, and I readily recognized my father and my best friend—as well as other entities—as discreet beings, too. It seems like a paradox, but in that realm it didn't feel paradoxical. It all fused together seamlessly. It was sort of like looking at the color red in the visible light spectrum where an infinite number of colors all flow as one ribbon. We can see that red is not orange or yellow, but the exact place where one begins and the other ends is imperceptible. There's no way to precisely separate the colors. That's how it seemed there. I was unique and recognizable, as were all others, yet there was no separation between us.

"When we come into our bodies, we have consciousness *and* we have an ego," I continued. "That's why we call this a state of duality. But in the state of non-duality, we are pure consciousness—that is, there's only oneness. And in that state, we cannot know personal pleasure as a discrete experience because there is no pain separate from all other emotions or experiences. We cannot know joy as a separate emotion because there is no suffering experienced as a unique phenomenon. In the nonphysical realm, what we experience is unconditional love—the combination of all emotions and experiences of everyone and everything in existence. Unconditional love is what radiates from universal oneness. But here in this physical world, we are able to feel joy only because we know what it means *not* to feel it. We feel pain because we also know what it means to be without pain. We have contrasting reference points.

"In the state of non-duality, there are no reference points. There is no opposite. There is only oneness and unconditional love, which means there is nothing outside of self. Everything *just is*. It felt to me like we actually *choose* to come here so we can experience a reality of separation—and an ego is absolutely necessary to feel this reality and to experience these feelings. Without an ego, we would be back to the state of non-duality, the state of oneness, of pure consciousness."

"I see what you're saying," Melissa interjected. "Most good plays and movies have a protagonist and an antagonist. If you only had one, without the other, then the audience wouldn't get to know the characters. If antagonists didn't have anyone to antagonize, you would not know them as antagonists, and vice versa. You need both to bring out the fullness of their personalities and their true nature."

Linda, who had been quiet most of this time, now spoke up. "I'm not sure that I'm convinced! My husband has a huge ego, and it drives me crazy! As far as he's concerned, he's always right! He always knows what's best for everyone, and he never apologizes for anything! It's always everyone else's fault! I would find it really hard to just sit by while he 'embraces his ego'!" Hearty laughter broke out at Linda's vehement outburst.

"Hey," Sally chimed in, "that sounds just like my husband, too!" We all laughed again.

"So, Linda, or Sally," I said, "if you were to address your husband about his ego, trying to get him to tone it down, how would you do it?"

"That's just it," Linda said with exasperation. "He refuses to acknowledge he has a huge ego! He can't see it! It's the rest of us who have to put up with it!"

"Just as I thought," I replied. "I've never met anyone who can see their own ego."

"So do you have any ideas on how to address people who have egos the size of a house?" Sally asked. "I can't even bear the thought of telling him to embrace his ego! He'd be incorrigible! He's bad enough as it is!" Once again the room filled with laughter, as many in the group started sharing stories of dealing with the overinflated egos of various people in their lives.

Ego and Awareness

"Okay, let's use our imagination a little bit here," I said, coming up with a metaphor to explain my understanding of the role of the ego. "Play along with me, and just imagine that we are all born with a remote control clutched in our little fists, and on that control are just two dials—nothing else. These two dials look sort of like the volume controls on old-fashioned radios, and the rim outside each dial is marked in increments from 0 to 10. But instead of volume, one of the dials is marked 'awareness' and the other one is marked 'ego.' And let's say that when we are born, both knobs are set to level 10. We come into this world with the intention of playing life at full volume. We come in predisposed to have both a healthy ego *and* a healthy sense of conscious awareness.

"Having the awareness level set to full blast means we are well aware of our connection with the universe and everyone and everything in it. I think we are indeed born knowing our deepest longings as well as the reasons why earth life has called to us, pulling us into this physical realm. And when we come here, at least for the first few years, we can still feel the connection with our loved ones in the nonphysical realm; we can hear their whispers inside our hearts, guiding us, imploring us not to forget who we are and where we came from.

"However, it isn't long before the noise of the outside world drowns out these inner whisperings, usually because of well-meaning (but sometimes not-so-well-meaning) people around us. Soon we start absorbing everyone else's fears as they misguidedly teach us how to survive and succeed in the '*real* world.' As they teach us how to succeed, they also discourage us from feeling empathy and connection with the rest of the world. They also make it clear that the realm from which we came and the connection we feel to it is a fantasy. So we start to tune out our awareness as we learn to navigate life on the physical realm. In other words, we start to turn down the volume of our conscious awareness.

"But as we turn down the awareness knob, our ego knob is still turned up full force. This makes our ego appear imbalanced with our level of awareness of others. And that's when we start to get accused of being egotistical—much like some of the people you are talking about," I added with a playful wink. "So it's not that they have huge egos or have become more egotistical. It's just that they *appear* that way because their conscious awareness knob is turned way down while their ego knob is still on full. That's very common, and it causes us to lose our connection with oneness. Our empathy for those around us is muted. We believe the ego is who we are.

"When I was growing up, I would always hear well-meaning people tell me not to be egotistical or ego driven. And especially in my culture, as a girl and later a woman, I was told I always had to suppress and control my ego. I was always discouraged from expressing my individuality. I was not supposed to be more suc-cessful or more popular or smarter than any man I might one day marry; and if I *were* popular or successful or smart, it would be hard to find a husband. In my culture, women are judged harshly if they aren't married by a certain age. So consequently, in order to appease those around me and fit in—and because of my fears of being judged—I turned the ego knob down almost to zero.

"As a result, both my knobs were turned down really low and I was operating at a fraction of the volume that I came into this life with. I wasn't expressing myself fully or allowing myself to be who I came here to be. I treated myself like a doormat and allowed others to do the same. I was so afraid of being judged and labeled egotistical that I made sure I put myself last. I made myself small so others could be big. Over the years, the suppression of my true self manifested as cancer."

First, Know Thyself

"This is why, as with the awareness knob, I believe that turning down the ego knob works to our detriment," I continued. "Not that I think everyone who doesn't express himself or herself fully is going to get cancer—far from it. But the ego helps us identify who we are and why we are here. No one can know our own self better than we can. Only we have access to the very deepest part of our being, the part of us that truly knows who we are, why we are here, and what we need to function at our best. In fact, knowing this greatly reduces much of the trauma and drama we create in constantly trying to please everyone, losing ourselves in the process.

"Yet society discourages us from asking these questions and exploring who we are. Once we start going to school, most of us are taught that indulging in self-exploration is a waste of time and a luxury because it's egotistical to take such an interest in ourselves. The result is that many of us who do feel a desire to deepen our knowledge of self soon drop the notion for fear of being judged. And so we continue to turn down our ego knob, thereby suppressing who we came here to be and becoming more and more out of balance."

"Thanks for that explanation," Henry piped up. "I get it now that both ego and awareness are necessary, and we have to turn them both up to have the full experience of life!" He looked genuinely pleased, and I felt good that I had been able to explain it to him.

"I believe that becoming self-aware is the most important thing we can do for ourselves . . . and for others!" I continued. "Knowing ourselves means to know what makes us happy—and what doesn't. It means having sufficient awareness to choose a path that will lead us to a greater sense of love and well-being. It also means being aware that we are far more expansive, more powerful, and more magnificent than what we have ever been led to believe. And when we fully know and love ourselves, we are then able to pass on this love and awareness to others. Bringing our fully realized, joyful, full-volume, well-cared-for self wherever we go—rather than offering a fearful, needy, or dysfunctional self—is the best thing we can do for ourselves as well as for everyone else."

In that moment, I noticed that the room was so completely silent that you could have heard a pin drop—everyone seemed totally riveted by our conversation. The only other sound in the room was the crackling of the fire in the fireplace.

"Currently, it can feel like we live in a world full of people who believe they are powerless, weak, and fearful—especially if you watch the news on television! And because this is what they believe they are, this is who they present when they go out and share themselves with the world. Most people have never been encouraged to truly get to know who they are, with both knobs at full volume," I continued.

"So Linda, going back to your point about dealing with people who have huge egos: If someone has a high ego volume, making them appear to be overly egotistical, they just need to be encouraged to turn up the volume on their awareness to balance the tone and allow them to feel connected with everyone else again. Instead of chiding them to 'turn down their ego,' simply encourage them to ramp up their awareness of self and others."

"That makes sense," said Linda. "But how can I do that?"

"Maybe start by asking your husband what makes him happy, or what would truly take his breath away. Ask him what he would do if he could do anything—where would he go? What dreams does he have that have not yet been fulfilled? Ask him what his fears are, too. If it seems too much of a stretch to just ask him these questions out of the blue, then perhaps start by saying you want to make some time each week to have a date night with him. Then schedule one evening where you both turn off all your electronic devices and commit to just bonding over conversation—and then use that opportunity to ask him the questions I just posed.

"To ease into it even more," I added, "start by telling him what you see as his positive qualities and what you love about him. And then share *your* dreams and aspirations with *him*, and tell him what *you* find fun and what brings you joy and makes you happy. He will then be more open to sharing his thoughts and feelings with you.

"If you know something about his life that you know has affected him—for example, maybe his mother died recently—perhaps gently bring it up and talk to him about his feelings around that. You could say something like, 'I really miss having her around. I think of her sometimes. Do you? I'll bet you must miss her too!'

"Remember, if his ego dial is turned up high, and his awareness dial is turned way down, you will have to tread gently and ease into these conversations lightly. But over time, and with patience, you can most definitely do it. And believe me, *it's worth it*!"

"That's really helpful," Linda said excitedly. "I think I can manage that! You've given me something to look forward to doing when I get home!"

Guiding Children and Teens

"What about kids? Would the same apply to them?" This time it was Shondra asking the questions. "My two teenagers are totally egotistical! It's all about 'me, me, me!' Would I use the same method to encourage awareness with them?"

"Children have an easier time with this because they haven't been here that long, so they are closer to who they truly came here to be," I started to explain. "Helping kids to turn up their awareness dial is actually a lot of fun. When younger ones talk about their imaginary friends or their deceased grandma visiting them, don't discourage them or tell them it's their imagination. Young children have very high suggestibility, which means that if you tell them what they're experiencing is not true and that it's just their imagination, they will take what you say to heart, and then that belief you give them will actually block them from having these kinds of experiences. After all, who are we to say it's not true? It may not be their imagination at all. They may truly be sensing their loved ones guiding them and communicating with them.

"For teenagers, I'd suggest making a project or a game out of it. Let's say you're out shopping for groceries with your kids, and you see someone in a wheelchair. Once you're sure you're out of earshot of that person, ask your teenager to think about what it would be like to manage everyday activities, like getting in the car, going shopping, taking a shower, or even going to the bathroom. You can go as deep as you like in this conversation, maybe even suggest your teenager write about it, or even better, try it out for themselves—even if only for a day or so! And then watch how your kid starts to think up creative ways of making the world easier to navigate for people who are confined to wheelchairs. It doesn't matter if what they think up sounds too crazy to be practical—the point is that it encourages them to dial up their awareness of others.

"On another day, if you see a homeless person, ask your teenager what they think it would feel like to have no money, to be hungry, and to have no home and no shelter from the elements. Once again, get your child to go deep and maybe even write about how they would feel, what would they do, and how would they survive. You might even ask them if they would like to try going a day or two with very little food so they could experience what it feels like to actually feel hunger.

"There are so many other conversations like this you can have with kids. Another example would be to ask them what it would feel like to be the kid at school who's always bullied and picked on for being different. Watch how your child's awareness toward others who would normally be outside their sphere of awareness starts to grow. Your child will develop the ability to feel what others feel, and you will have a really sensitive and aware child who will be the first one to stand up for the underdog!"

"That's a great way of doing it!" Shondra said. "Why don't schools incorporate this kind of thinking into their teaching instead of constantly pushing kids to compete with each other and fear those who are different?"

"Be careful how you couch what you say," I added. "I'd never, ever tell a youngster, 'You should be more compassionate! Why don't you think about others? You are so selfish!' Kids hate being berated like that, and this will only push them away. That's the kind of thinking that was drilled into me when I was growing up.

Believing I was selfish dimmed my light and made me afraid to shine in this world. No one wants that for their children!"

"I'm so glad you explained everything about the ego," Jane chimed in. She had been quiet for a while. "People often have the expectation that spiritual teachers have transcended their egos, and then they judge them when they appear *not* to have transcended their egos. Not to mention that we judge ourselves whenever we see our own egos rearing its head. But now I can see that not only is it actually *not possible* to fully live in the physical world without an ego, but it's also actually *necessary* to have a strong, healthy ego. As long as we are here on earth, we need the ego for our own survival and to experience all the many things we have come here to experience—all the contrasting qualities that go into making up our reality here. That really makes sense to me."

"Yes," I replied. "The belief that we must suppress or control the ego is so pervasive in spiritual and religious communities that spiritual teachers can actually become afraid of disappointing people—afraid people will discover that they actually have an ego. But if we were to realize that we *all* have an ego and that our ego is an important and necessary part of our experience here, then we could breathe more comfortably and allow ourselves to be who we are, instead of trying to pretend we are something or someone we are not. The paradox is that once we accept and embrace the ego and understand what its purpose is, it stops being an issue! We become transparent, and we no longer need to feed, suppress, or deny our egos. In fact, we can *enjoy* them in a way that's healthy for ourselves and for everyone around us!

Be the God That You Are

"You keep mentioning that we need to know who and what we truly are," said James, who in his mid-20s was the youngest in the group. "But what does that really mean? Who and what *are* we, in fact?"

"It's actually a lot simpler than it seems," I answered. "I wish kids were taught this when they're young. I wish *I* had been taught this instead of being encouraged to be competitive and to hide my true self. We only need to know that we are the divine manifesting through this body right now . . . that every single one of us is divinity expressing through our own eyes in our three-dimensional, physical world.

"When we are taught to be competitive—that is, that we have to get better grades than everyone else in order to get into better colleges and get better jobs because there isn't enough in this world to go around—in essence, what we are being told is that we are separate. I have to be better than you in order to make it. I have to fear you and feel that your success is a threat to my own success. Some people even take this to the extreme, and out of a fear of failing, they deliberately find ways to trip others up in order to get ahead themselves. This is a possible result of our awareness knob being turned right down to zero, while our ego knob is turned up full volume. In this situation, we have no awareness of the needs or feelings of others, nor do we sense our connection with others beyond our own needs and our own fears.

"But imagine if we were encouraged to keep our awareness knob turned up to full volume. And then imagine if we were taught to collaborate instead of compete. What a different world we would have. Were this to happen, I believe we would have much more compassion, respect, and love for the planet as a whole, as well as for its inhabitants."

Many nodded their heads in agreement. I'd clearly struck a chord. I paused a moment, because I wanted them to pay close attention to what I was about to share next because for me, it had been such a powerful lesson.

"I notice that when I remember who I truly am—that I am divinity expressing through this body, through this personality, this ego, this culture, this life—the people around me change and react to what I am feeling within myself," I continued. "My circumstances change, and my reactions to situations change. I believe that *each and every one of us* is powerful beyond belief, and none of us is deprived of this power. It's only our beliefs and our conditioning that blind us to the numinous, or universal force within. We are living and breathing our godhood all day, every day, even though we are often unaware of it. I'm not referring to the gods of organized religions here, so this is true even for someone who isn't religious or doesn't believe in any god at all. In that case, a person could just substitute whatever helps them realize the highest vision of their self."

Again, the room went silent. I could feel everyone taking this in, aware that this was an absolutely vital truth that could change everything if they'd allow it.

"One of the things I believe caused me to get cancer was that I had forgotten my godhood, my own divinity. I'd forgotten that I—along with everyone and everything in the universe—am the divine manifesting in this life. As a result, I was unable to choose paths that expanded my sense of well-being and my sense of happiness. Those paths were simply not available to me at the level I'd turned my awareness knob down to.

"Yet in the NDE realm, I suddenly remembered that all I had to do was to be myself and live my divine truth. I simply had to know *with every cell of my being* that I am the divine manifesting in this world, and that just by being myself, I was the personification of this truth—one of the myriad ways divinity becomes manifest in this life. Even if I remind myself of this fact 100 times a day, it cannot be too much. You and I are the numinous expressing through these bodies, at this time and place, right here, right now. There can be no more important awareness than this."

Come for the Ego, Stay for the Life

"This sounds really amazing!" Deborah said. "But if it's so amazing to have our awareness knob turned full on, and it seems to help us remember who we are and where we came from and what we came here for, then I can't see anything wrong with turning our ego knob down. What harm can that do? Surely it would make us better people."

"I can see how having high awareness and low ego would *appear* to make us better people, at least as far as how it would affect others. However, I don't think you could survive in the world that way. To me, the ego is part of our survival mechanism," I explained. "With full awareness, and no ego, it would be exactly like the state I was in during my NDE. In that realm, without my physical body, it was difficult to separate my own identity, my own emotions, and so on, from anything else. I felt everyone's emotions as strongly as my own. I felt the pain of the one who was hurt as well as the one who did the hurting due to their own pain and lack of love.

"So in that state, I couldn't discern between 'bad' and 'good' because there *was* no 'bad' and 'good.' I felt empathy and compassion for every single creature on the planet and nothing but unconditional love for everybody, even those who had hurt me, because I understood that they had done so because of their own ignorance or suffering. It's hard to stay immersed in that state while living in this world, because we are dealing with other people all the time, in every aspect of our lives. It would make you very vulnerable. You'd be a target for those with full-on egos because all you would feel for them is unconditional love, and you would feel all of their pain, all of the time. You would need some kind of mechanism to help you survive as an individual, otherwise you would get completely lost in the demands, pain, and emotions of everyone else. Amazingly there *is* just such a mechanism in place for us in the physical world—and that mechanism is called the ego!"

Several in the group chuckled, and many nodded their heads as this realization sunk in.

"Perhaps if everyone else also had their ego dials turned down and lived from their conscious awareness," piped up James, "it would be easier to do the same."

"Maybe that's the idea behind ashrams and communes," Shondra suggested. "To create a community where we leave the ego behind and everyone comes together on purely a conscious awareness level. But then, why come to this earth at all? Why not just stay in the state of non-duality rather than come to a place where ego is so important?"

"Although communes and ashrams are a good concept for conscious living, it doesn't always work out as intended," Kathy added. "I think people being people, they bring their egos everywhere they go. I have been to an ashram where, although it was great for the most part, the longer I was there, the more I noticed everyone's egos starting to come out. The people were as competitive there as they are in the outside world. They were even competitive about their spiritual learning. Each one wanted to prove to the guru that they were more spiritual than the others! Not to mention that they were all vying for attention from the guru—they all wanted to be the teacher's pet. And one time, when the guru didn't get exactly what he had requested from the disciples who take care of his needs, I saw even him get short with them and dress them down!"

"I think that when we deny the ego, it kind of pops out unannounced and uncontrolled in all sorts of situations, I suggested. "On the other hand, if we just embrace the ego and acknowledge its existence—acknowledge it as an important part of why we came into this life in the first place—then it doesn't need to keep surprising us by exploding at the most inopportune moments! I honestly think that it's extremely difficult to live in this realm without an ego—which is probably why those who truly strive to live purely from conscious awareness, wanting no involvement from their ego, end up living reclusive lives, much like hermits."

"Can you imagine two people in a relationship where one has their ego dialed way up and their awareness dialed down, while their partner has it the other way around?" James asked. "Just think about what *that* would be like!"

"Wow," Kathy said. "I'll bet the one with the full-on ego will be calling all the shots in the relationship, while the other one will be doing all the running around, indulging them!"

"If we don't have an ego," I added, "then it's not possible to meet our own needs. And then we are opening ourselves up to being abused by others. This is why it's important to love our self—and to have an ego!"

As if on cue, the manager of the hotel appeared to announce that the tractor driver had arrived to take us across the water to the mainland. He was expecting us to cheer at being "rescued," but what he heard instead was a chorus of "Aww, so soon?" But sure enough, two whole hours had passed, and it was now almost

6 P.M.! We finished the last sips of our tea, gathered our things, and made our way out of the hotel and down the path toward the beach, where our chariot awaited.

One by one, we climbed up the ladder along the side of the water tractor to the raised platform. As the vehicle chugged to the beach on the mainland, we looked out to the expansive ocean. Once there, we hopped off and walked back along the sand and up the rocky steps to the spot where our bus was waiting to take us back to the college. Everyone was in a buoyant mood as we headed off to Dartington. Being stranded had been such an unexpected treat—a totally unscheduled and impromptu opportunity for a great discussion!

I knew the rest of the retreat would provide a much deeper experience for everyone, now that we'd had a chance to examine just why it is that we need our egos here in the physical world— not to mention how to keep them in balance with our awareness that we are truly all connected, part of one whole. And once again, I was struck by how much our experience of the physical plane is enriched when we learn to love ourselves and honor the part that we have each come here to play in this realm.

Living Heaven *Here and Now*

If "Being spiritual means overcoming the ego" is a *myth*, then what could be the *truth*?

Consider These Possible Truths

- The ego is not our enemy, and we don't need to overcome it; the ego is necessary for survival in the physical world.

- We choose to come into the physical realm to experience separation and duality with all the rich, contrasting qualities that make up

reality here; without the ego, this experience
would be impossible.

- We are born predisposed to have both a
healthy ego *and* a healthy sense of conscious
awareness.

- Loving ourselves is not being egotistical; it's
absolutely vital to our optimal health and
happiness.

- The more we love ourselves and embrace
our ego, the easier it becomes for us to see
ourselves beyond our ego and to become
aware of our infinite selves.

Tips and Exercises

- Reflect on how you live your life and interact
with others, including your thoughts and
emotions. Begin to discern where on the scale
you have tuned both your awareness knob
and your ego knob.

- If you have a loved one whose ego knob is
out of balance with their awareness knob,
encourage them to dial up their awareness
by gently asking them questions about their
dreams, their aspirations, and even their fears
while sharing your own.

- Keep a record, perhaps in your journal, of
when you were able to remain aware of your
divine nature and how others reacted and
responded, as well as of when you forgot your
connection to the divine, and how others
reacted and responded to that. Compare the
two experiences.

- Each time you feel anxiety, fear, or even
anger remind yourself that nothing (and no

one) can deprive you of the God-force that lives within you, and that feeding that God-force with self-love and self-care instead of feeding your fears and negative emotions will help you connect with your true God-nature more readily.

Questions to Ask Yourself

- Do I suppress my desires and the expression of my true self because I'm afraid of being judged? Do I always put myself last?

- What would it be like for me to remain keenly aware of my connection to everyone around me and to want to collaborate with others instead of compete?

- Have I allowed others' judgments to dilute my awareness, turn down my volume, and encourage me to act as though I'm far less than I actually am?

- What beliefs do I have that keep me from realizing that I am one of many expressions of God in this physical world? What would it take to dissolve the beliefs and conditioning that keep me from fully accepting my true nature?

I know I am in balance, operating with both my ego knob and my awareness knob turned full-on, when . . .

- I have compassion and empathy for others without taking on the heavy mantle of everyone's pain as if all of it were my own.

- I am grateful for my ego because it allows me to express my uniqueness and discover who I am and why I chose to be here in the physical realm.

- I don't judge others (including spiritual teachers) for not having transcended their egos.

- I understand that when others have hurt me, they've done so because of their own ignorance or suffering.

- I show up as my fully realized, joyful self (instead of projecting a fearful, needy, or dysfunctional version of myself), knowing that this not only empowers me, but also everyone I come in contact with.

MYTH:
WOMEN ARE THE
WEAKER SEX

"Can you sign this book to 'Samirah'?" asked a beautiful olive-skinned woman with large dark eyes looking out at me from under her hijab (the traditional covering for the hair and neck worn by Muslim women). She was the final person standing in the book-signing line at a Hay House event in Pasadena, California, where I had just finished speaking.

"Sure," I responded. "That's a beautiful name!"

"Thank you. It's my name," she said with a smile, proceeding to spell it out to ensure that I wrote it correctly.

"I loved your book," she continued, as I inscribed a message for her on the title page. "I related to so much of your life story, especially some of the cultural challenges."

"Cultural challenges can be *so* tricky!" I responded. "I'm so glad I don't have to deal with most of that anymore!"

"You're so lucky," she said. "In fact, do you have time to talk? I waited to be the last in line just to see if you could give me a few minutes of your time. Let me buy you a cup of tea or coffee."

I looked at Samirah's perfectly chiseled and smiling face, her lovely silk hijab falling softly around the shoulders of her dark floral dress, which reached below her ankles. Instinctively sensing the potential for an extremely interesting conversation, I accepted her invitation. I then glanced over my shoulder at Jennifer, the Hay House employee who helps make my life easier at all my speaking engagements.

"I'm fine from here, Jen!" I said. "Thanks for all your help!"

"You sure you're okay?" she asked. "Do you want me to walk you to the authors' lounge?"

"No, I'm fine. I'm going to have a cup of tea with this lovely woman," I responded, gesturing at Samirah and then reaching over to give Jen a hug to show my appreciation for all her help.

"There's a quiet café just down the hallway of the convention center," Samirah mentioned. "I had my lunch there earlier."

"Everyone's gone into the auditorium to listen to the next speaker," I said "so I think we'll have the place to ourselves."

We made our way there, and after we sat down and ordered our tea, Samirah jumped right in with her first question.

"When you talk about being in the other realm, you always say that you were without your culture, your gender, your religion, and so on. Are you sure about this?" she asked intently. "I mean, are we all *really* without our gender, our culture, and our religion when we die?" She seemed desperate for assurance.

Heaven Has No Gender

"Yes, absolutely!" I responded. "We have no physical bodies in the other realm, and gender is part of our physical bodies. It's part of our biology because in this realm, we are expected to pro-create—so we must have reproductive systems. But when we are without our bodies, we have no need for a reproductive system. We have no biology, as such. We are pure spirit, just beings of light—pure essence, pure consciousness."

"I completely believe you. But the problem is that I live in a culture that is run by men. We women are invisible. It doesn't matter how smart I am or how much knowledge I have. I have to give in to men on every issue, just because they are men, regardless of their position, their personal experience, or their education," Samirah shared.

"In order to be valued in my culture, I have to be subservient and dim my light! The more invisible I am, the more I make myself small, the more the man in my life can be big—and then the more valuable I become! I have to do the *opposite* of what you say we have come here to do. To be valued, I am *expected* to have all those traits you *used* to have before you got cancer! They are seen as positive traits for women in my culture.

"One time, I completely locked horns with my husband on an issue having to do with our daughter and some problems she was having at school," Samirah continued. "She was struggling, trying to fit in, but my husband didn't want her to integrate into a foreign culture, even though he was the one who made the decision to move out of our country and live here because of his business! It broke my heart to see her struggle so much, trying to negotiate cultures. My son didn't have the same problems because my husband allowed him to integrate into the local culture, making friends with the local boys at school and doing the things they do. My husband is much more lenient with him than he is with our daughter.

"He wouldn't budge on this issue, and I was certain that what I wanted to do was best for her. So I went to see a well-respected man in our community whom we often go to for advice. I thought he would understand the issue because he has lived in the U.S. for a long time and has raised a family here. I was hoping he would help me to speak with my husband. But after I told him the issue, his response was, 'You must listen to your husband, because after all, he is the man of the house. It isn't right to go against his wishes, and it's not right to encourage your daughter to go against his wishes. You have to explain that to your daughter, otherwise how will she ever learn that this is our culture? Since we are not living in our home country, she is not learning about her culture at school. So it's your responsibility to teach her. She will have to adjust to her own husband some day. It's better that she start learning now, or she (and you) will have problems when she is of marriageable age! It will be difficult for her to find a suitable husband if she strays too far from our traditions.' Can you imagine my frustration when he responded in that way?"

"I can *completely* understand how frustrating that must have been for you!" I answered, remembering many of the cultural issues I had faced, trying to fit in with my school friends and wishing that I did not have to deal with trying to stay within my cultural restrictions. I had been given the same warning—that if I strayed too far from our cultural norms, I would have a very hard time finding a husband!

"I've read your book, as well as the accounts of many others who have had experiences like yours," Samirah continued. "So for me, the proverbial veil has been pulled back. I feel I can see the truth. Your experience in particular really hit home for me because of the cultural issues you had faced. I *know* what you say is true. But knowing that, how can I ever fit in again? I now struggle seeing the blatant gender disparity that takes place all around me. I recognize how women have been silenced and overpowered in my culture, and how in our silence, those with the loudest voices have taken control. It's not that anything around me is different or has changed. It's *me* who has changed. My world has blown wide open because I now know that this is *not* how God intended it to be for us women. We are all equal in the eyes of God. All our voices matter just the same. And it's the louder, more aggressive male voices among us that have created this false perception of women. But why does it feel as though only *I* am seeing it this way? A part of me wonders: *Was I better off not knowing?*"

Gender Roles Are Cultural

What Samirah was telling me was so raw and so powerful. I really felt for her, and her words deeply resonated with me because I totally related to them. The timing of this encounter was interesting because I had recently been thinking about the gender disparity and how it affects our society. I had been watching the coverage of the 2016 presidential race on television, and it struck me as very unusual that until this election, no woman had ever before become a serious candidate for nomination in a country much of the world considers to be one of the most progressive and freest on the planet. To top it off, the candidates' debate I'd been watching most recently (the first Republican debate) featured 10 men but not a single woman (although one woman relegated to a secondary debate improved her polling numbers enough to be included in subsequent main debates). The candidates had been discussing sensitive issues, such as whether a woman should have the legal right to abort the fetus if she were to become pregnant. They went on to discuss the topic of rape and whether a woman had the legal right to abortion if she were raped. I found it disturbing that an overwhelming number of these candidates declared that they were against abortion under *any* circumstances, even if the pregnancy was caused by rape!

What was even more disturbing was that their decisions directly affected women's bodies and women's lives, much more so than the men who impregnated those women, *yet no woman was being consulted on this issue.*

As I watched this, my mind was flooded with memories of growing up in Asia and being indoctrinated in a culture where all the dominant roles were male. And I was now hit with the realization that it wasn't just *my* culture that was this way. It was largely the same the world over. Some cultures are just more overt about this than others.

Although no one actually verbalized this, it was clear to me from the time I was very young that women always held roles that were subservient to or in some way served men. It seemed almost normal for men to dominate. This myth, like any other, informed my thinking well into my 20s because this seemed to be true in real life as well as on television. All the senior roles in the corporate world, in government, in politics, in the armed forces, and so on were held by men; and if women were in the picture at all, they had supporting roles such as a junior clerical assistant, stenographer, or secretary.

Doctors were more often than not depicted as men, and their nurses were women. My kindergarten and elementary school teachers were always women, but as we went higher into our senior years and college, they were mostly men. This went on and on.

"Samirah, you probably already know from reading my book that I grew up in a culture where arranged marriages are the norm, and I spent my youth being groomed to be a wife," I said after taking a long sip of my tea.

"Yes, I know, but I think the community I have been brought up in is much more orthodox than the one you were brought up in," she said. "You have no idea how lucky you are that your parents still accepted you after you came back from running away from the arranged marriage all those years ago, and that you later married a wonderful man who understands and supports you and your ideals—especially after having such a life-transforming experience! My situation is similar, yet very different! My father was very strict and very proud. We couldn't go against his wishes, no matter *what* the reason!"

Although my parents were very loving as I was growing up, their gender roles were clearly defined by our culture. My dad went to work, and my mom took care of our home and the kids. Dad always had the last word on all the major decisions for our family, and even though my mother knew how to get her way sometimes, she had to be really creative in finding ways to make my father see her point of view. Creativity and timing was everything for her, and getting him to agree with her was a victory, whereas we all took for granted that my dad had ultimate power to veto anything. In other words, their relationship was not built on mutual trust and equality but on traditional cultural roles for men and women.

Culture Is Not Ultimate Reality

"So please tell me," Samirah asked emphatically, "what was it like when you first came back from your NDE? What was it like after you realized the truth but had to come back and live in this world?"

"Oh, Samirah, it wasn't easy!" I answered. "When I came out of my coma and healed from the cancer, I wanted to shout what I had learned from the rooftops! I felt I had seen beyond the veil, and now knew who I truly was! I believed that I had discovered something that would help all of us see that none of us is less than anyone or anything else! I felt I had finally seen the truth and that others would be interested to know what I had discovered.

"I soon realized that the world was not ready for this truth, however, because so much of what I had to say went against many of our cultural norms. And I had to accept that much of what I was saying would be seen as a threat to traditional beliefs. I couldn't shout it from the rooftops, even though I felt I had no choice but to share, which I knew was the reason I had come back. So I shared in the relative safety of obscure chat groups on the Internet while I went about quietly living my life.

"But the universe was determined that I share my story in a bigger way," I continued. "I was *meant* to shout it from the rooftops! That was what my dad and my best friend meant when I met them in the other realm and they said, 'Go back and live your life fearlessly!' I realized this after my story went viral on the Internet, and then Wayne Dyer found me and encouraged me to write a book. I felt as though the universe was pulling my story out of me so I could spread it fearlessly. As a result, I have found a new place in the world, and I now have a platform where I can freely share my voice and my views."

"But it must have been so strange when you first came back to be able to see how so much of what you were brought up to believe was not true," Samirah replied. "That must have felt quite scary."

"It was more than scary. I felt lonely!" I said. "When I was in the other realm I could see so clearly how I had bought into all the various beliefs handed to me as I was growing up—including those based on tradition, superstition, or misinformation that are passed down from generation to generation without anyone ever questioning them. I also understood that until we actually believe in those myths, they have no power. *Our belief* in them is what makes them true for us. And many of the myths we buy into are unhealthy." As I poured some more tea into my cup, I could see that Samirah was listening intently.

"It is almost impossible to step out of ourselves and view these invisible beliefs because it would be like the eye trying to view itself without a mirror, or the tip of your finger trying to touch itself with the same finger," I continued. "So it wasn't until I was outside my physical body—as well as outside of my earthly *persona*—that I could recognize that everything in my life that had made me feel less than, smaller than, or weaker than another was simply not true!"

"Thank you *so much* for explaining this so clearly," Samirah said with great relief. "I get it. But I want to know one more thing: Why would we choose to come here as women if we are going to be treated as inferior or weaker?"

"There is a reason you came as the person you did, in your particular family, with your particular husband and your children, and in your particular culture," I said. "That's what it felt like for me, anyway. I believe that we all have a reason for being male, female, or even transgendered—and that there's even a reason for being gay or straight. I believe we are born knowing the truth of who we are, and we come here with the hope of sharing this truth with others. But most of us slowly start to forget that truth as we become conditioned to integrate into our surrounding culture. We fall into the trap of not wanting to disappoint those around us, so we dim our light to fit in."

Yin and Yang

"Of course, in the other realm, women are not seen as weaker than men," I added. "Remember, when we are without our bodies, we are all equal and we are all equally powerful. Think of the terms *yin* and *yang*, the Chinese symbols for feminine and masculine energy, respectively. Together, yin and yang make a complete circle—both are needed to complete it. That's how it's seen from the other realm, not just with gender but with *everything*. All contrasting values go into making a complete whole.

"I believe that we choose to come here either as a man or a woman, or even transgendered, depending on what we want to experience. So if we choose to be a woman, then we typically have more yin energy. This means we are more in tune with nature and our emotions, as well as with the emotions of others. Being more yin also makes us more maternal, nurturing, and empathic. But if we choose to be born a man, then we typically have more yang energy. This more often makes us more outwardly focused and physically stronger, faster, bigger—traits that make us better protectors. This generally holds true even if the body we are born into has a different gender from the gender we chose to come in with. Ultimately, our energy matches who we truly are—not necessarily our physical bodies—although of course we choose those physical bodies just like we choose our culture, even if they don't 'match' what is true for us.

"Yin and yang are complementary, not opposing, forces. They interact to form a dynamic system in which the whole is greater than the individual parts. *Everything* has both yin and yang aspects. For instance, shadow cannot exist without light. In the same way, we humans cannot exist without both male and female to perpetuate the species. If we were to wipe out either women or men, we would wipe out the entire human race in one generation!"

"Then why can't men see that?" Samirah asked emphatically.

"Actually, I don't think it's just the men," I responded. "I think we are *all* complicit in allowing this to happen and perpetuating it. For example, when I was growing up, if I did anything that went against my culture—if I dressed inappropriately or was caught coming home too late at night—the men weren't the only ones who were talking about me; the women did, too! The mothers of adult sons in our community would shame me by telling my mother that I was not good enough to marry their sons because I was sure to be sullied if I was dating and going out at night!"

As I said this last bit, I waved my index finger in front of Samirah's face in a mocking gesture, as though pointing a finger at her shameful behavior. We looked at each other and burst out laughing—we both knew *exactly* the sort of social pressure that came from this sort of shaming.

"I've also been following the current situation in India with the high number of rape cases publicized there," I continued in a more serious tone. "Rape happens all the time in India, but mostly rapes go unreported because the culture blames the victim, who is seen as bringing shame to her family. In many cases, it's not just men but also women who accuse victims of 'asking for it' by being dressed in a provocative way or staying out so late at night.

"Rape, under any circumstances, should not be tolerated, so it saddens me that anyone—let alone women—can blame victims for being raped. I think we as women need to defend these girls. We also must teach our sons to respect and protect those who are physically weaker, and that not only is it abhorrent to rape and abuse women, but so is tolerating those who do!"

"I agree," Samirah said. "I know that in my culture, we generally try to control our daughters instead of teaching our sons how to respect and care for women. I don't know why we do that!"

"I think it's because that is the way people have been for generations," I responded. "And I want to be clear here that in no way am I blaming any one gender for the predicament we find ourselves in! On the contrary! It's just that there is no excuse for anyone to perpetrate these heinous acts, and it's abhorrent that any person from a civilized society would condone the use of their strength to abuse those who are physically weaker. But I don't want to go down the road of playing the blame game, as that leads nowhere. As a society or culture, we all need to take responsibility for our part in enabling these acts to take place. That is so much more empowering than sitting around waiting for things to change.

"One of the challenges many societies face," I continued, "is that they have almost no role models for women moving freely in the world. Even today, women are still depicted in the shadow of men, and those women who are progressive and want to improve their life feel they have to fight in a man's world, which is truly unfortunate. Having to constantly fight in order to preserve their sense of dignity and freedom forces women to suppress their feminine qualities and become more like men to succeed. And while we may admire women who do this from a distance, most of us are afraid to do the same. Most women don't have the courage to compete on male terms because they know they are going to be judged as being too ballsy, too bossy, too aggressive. Many women worry that it would make them less attractive as partners."

Gentle Is Strong

"I remember in my last job, before my illness, I had climbed the corporate ladder and had reached a glass ceiling," I recalled. "I realized I couldn't go any further. All the people at the top were men, and I just knew they were not going to let me go any higher, even though I worked really hard and had wonderful relationships with all my clients. I met my targets and was doing really well. But when I was up for promotion, I was passed over for a man! And my boss told me that I wouldn't be able to be promoted any higher.

"I wanted to know why, and he pretty much told me it was because I was a woman. And since I was married, he added, I was going to be distracted by my husband, maybe have kids, and so on. Not only did he make it clear that I would not be promoted, but he also alluded to the fact that he would have no problem demoting me at any point if I was going to be a 'typical woman' and let my marriage and home life distract me!

"For a while, I tried really hard to be tough and strong, to prove to him that I could do the job as well as any man. I endured long hours and stressful work in an environment dominated by men, trying hard not to look like a 'typical woman.' But I could tell that he didn't like the fact that I was doing so well, because he didn't want me to be 'one of the boys' in the senior management team. Several times, he deliberately set me up to fail by constantly increasing my targets to unrealistic levels and then reporting to the head office that I wasn't meeting those goals.

"When I would voice my concern about such treatment, he would tell me that I was too sensitive and needed to toughen up if I wanted to move up the corporate ladder! At first, I would beat myself up, scolding myself for being so sensitive. I was afraid my boss would demote me for being weak, so I tried to suppress all my feminine qualities and 'man up.' But after a while, I became exhausted, stressed, and so burned out that I finally resigned! At that time, I felt a lot of anger toward my boss because I knew he had deliberately manipulated me.

"It wasn't until my experience in the other realm that I came to the realization that I *am* a typical woman and that I should be *proud* of it! What's wrong with having 'typical' feminine qualities? They are some of my greatest strengths! I shouldn't need to become more like a man to succeed in this world. In fact, I was deserving of success *because* of these qualities, not *despite* them!"

Samirah agreed with enthusiasm: "We need to step out and become leaders, but on *our* terms, not on men's terms. We need to form our own businesses, our own companies, where both male and female energies can coexist harmoniously. We need to see our sensitivity as our strength, not as a weakness. We need to allow our empathy, our hearts, and our compassion to take center stage instead of hiding them so we can compete in a 'man's world.'"

"*Yes!*" I exclaimed. "This is the mistake we make, both as men and as women, and it's one of the big reasons why our world is so imbalanced. We've bought into the myth that feminine qualities are weaker qualities and that we need to bury them in order to succeed at a career—when actually, they are anything *but* weak, and they deserve respect. Both masculine and feminine are needed to make a healthy whole! In fact, to become the healthiest society possible, we need to think in terms of liberation for everyone, whether man, woman, transgendered, gay, straight—irrespective of a person's race or socioeconomic level.

"You might be interested to know that after I left that job I told you about, my boss struggled because I was the one who had maintained all the relationships with our clients. My company was a wholesaler of women's fashion accessories, and my clients had trusted me to order all the right products for their stores because I seemed to have a knack for choosing styles that suited Asian women. I had bonded with all of the buyers. When my boss was left to deal with them on his own, he had no clue what to order for them. He had no relationship with them, so they weren't loyal to him. They weren't happy that he had let me go, and they moved on to other brands. What he didn't realize when he threatened to demote me was that the clients were loyal to *me*, not to the product. In the end, the company lost so much money that the people at the head office fired my boss and sold his division."

Samirah chuckled at the irony of my story before her expression turned serious.

"I'm glad he learned his lesson that just because you weren't a typical businessman doesn't mean you didn't add immense value to the business!" she said. "This sort of situation happens the world over. When a woman gets overpowered *just because she is a woman*, it is to the detriment of not only that one woman, but also of *everyone*, including society in general."

"Yes, I agree, but I do think this is slowly changing and that we're making at least *some* progress," I replied. "We need both men and women to allow this progress to continue if we are to overcome the imbalance society has created, and as you said, this will be for the betterment of *all* of us."

"I completely agree with you, Anita!" Samirah said, grinning from ear to ear. "I feel so hopeful talking about this with you, even though none of my own problems have been solved!"

"I know, I was just thinking that," I responded. "We've just solved the problems of the world, but we haven't made a dent in your personal situation!"

At that we both started laughing again with great pleasure.

"But *you* have a voice now," Samirah said, wide-eyed with excitement. "You have been given a platform from which to express yourself and a stage to shout from. Use it! You must talk about *everything* we've just been discussing!"

"I will," I assured her.

"I really get it now! It's not about blaming anyone—men or women," Samirah said. "Instead, it's about all of us coming together and starting to take responsibility for our part in the world we have created—especially if we want a better, more balanced world for ourselves and our kids. Even if my husband won't change or won't see things this way, my kids don't have to continue to perpetuate this harmful myth in the next generation.

That's the reason why I see through the myth, because at least in my family, it stops with me—it's up to me to teach my children the truth."

"Exactly!" I said with great enthusiasm. "Busting this myth means teaching our sons to treat women the way we want our daughters to be treated, instead of attempting to control our daughters and then blaming them when they're disrespected or mistreated by men. And you never know, Samirah—your husband may someday learn something from your kids! It happens, you know! It's not too late!"

"I really would love for that to happen," Samirah said hopefully.

"By the way, can I share our conversation in my next book?" I asked.

"Yes, absolutely! In fact, you *must* share it!" she responded, asking me not to use her real name. I assured her I wouldn't and then glanced down at my watch to discover that it was much later than I expected. The time I spent with Samirah had just flown by!

"Samirah, I have to run or I'll miss my ride back to the hotel!" I told her.

"I so enjoyed just sitting and chatting with you!" she said as I stood up. "What a lovely conversation—thank you *so* much!"

"I enjoyed it every bit as much as you did, and you gave me another chapter for my next book, so for that I thank *you!*" I said, laughing as we hugged each other tightly and then parted company.

Samirah headed toward the main entrance of the building, and I walked to the authors' lounge in back of the stage. I will think of this conversation for a long time and know that Samirah and I will continue to be in each other's thoughts often as we go about our separate, yet connected, journeys.

Living Heaven *Here and Now*

If "Women are the weaker sex" is a *myth*, then what could be the *truth*?

Consider These Possible Truths

- Neither gender is superior to or inferior to the other—each has important qualities that are needed to make a complete and balanced whole. That whole is not only much greater than the sum of its individual parts, but much grander than we can possibly comprehend.

- In the spirit realm, we have no physical bodies and so gender does not exist. We are all equal, and we are all equally powerful.

- We choose to be born into the physical realm as either a male or a female (including those who choose to be born transgendered), depending on what we want to experience in this life.

- We are born knowing the truth of who we are (including our gender and our sexuality) and with a desire to share this truth with others. As we grow up, we can easily forget that truth and become conditioned by society to "edit" our image (dimming our own light) to blend more easily into what society considers acceptable or desirable.

Tips and Exercises

- Make a commitment—whether you are a
  parent or not—to encourage children of
  both genders to feel empowered (including
  speaking up if and when anyone tries to
  intimidate them), as well as to encourage boys
  to respect girls (and vice versa). Model this
  behavior yourself.

- Notice how making that commitment
  and taking such steps, even if they are
  small at first, makes you feel like an active,
  empowered, and vital part of the solution
  rather than a passive observer or victim of
  society's status quo.

- If you are female, list your strongest feminine
  traits (such as sensitivity, intuitiveness,
  empathy, compassion, ability to nurture,
  and so on) and reflect on how they enable
  you to add light to the world and make
  valuable contributions. If you are male, list
  the strongest feminine traits of those women
  who are closest to you and reflect on what
  gifts those traits have brought you as well
  as others.

Questions to Ask Yourself

- What would it feel like to refuse to tolerate
  any act of sexism, violent or otherwise, that I
  witness—whether it is directed at me or not?
  How can I be part of the solution?

- In what subtle ways might I have
  automatically bought into society's views
  about women being inferior, possibly without
  even being aware of it?

- What empowering qualities do I hide—at least sometimes—in order to not attract too much attention or to keep others from feeling uncomfortable? How might my life be different if I felt proud of those qualities and free to show them all the time?

I know that I am not allowing my gender to determine my self-worth when . . .

- I do not allow people's opinions or beliefs about my biological sex, my gender, or my sexual orientation (as well as my race and socioeconomic level) to make me feel less than, smaller than, or weaker in any way.

- I refuse to tolerate or perpetuate any societal conditioning that insists one gender or sexual orientation is more desirable or superior. I am willing for the buck to stop with me.

- I take responsibility for the world that I have helped to create, not blaming others for how they may have contributed to the imbalances in that world. Instead I focus on helping to restore that balance, knowing that this will inspire others to have the courage to do the same.

MYTH:
WE MUST ALWAYS
BE POSITIVE

"**M**y young son died three months ago, and I want to know why he was taken away from me so soon! He was my only child, and he was my world! I am a single mother, and he was my reason for living!" The young woman was speaking into the microphone in a quavering voice, her eyes welling up with tears. "I cannot bear the thought that I will never see him again! I can't make sense of it and just don't know how I can keep on living!"

I was on a tour in Australia, speaking at an event near Brisbane. It was near the end of my presentation, the question-and-answer segment, which I usually enjoy very much. But as this grief-stricken mother waited for me to respond, with tears streaming down her cheeks, I found I was unable to speak. No words would come.

Although I knew from having directly experienced the other realm that her son was fine, I also sensed that assuring her of this truth didn't seem like enough—or even appropriate. The woman's words had pierced my heart to its center, and speech was simply impossible. All I could see and feel in that moment was her pain and loss. I became thoroughly enveloped by her suffering.

Time stood still. I all but forgot I was standing onstage in front of hundreds of people who were waiting for me to utter words of soothing consolation and love. No doubt they were wondering what kind of wisdom I was about to impart to help this grieving mother make sense of her dire situation and come to terms with her loss. Most likely, they were hopeful that my answer would also help them make sense of their own anguish and unresolved pain from the loss of a loved one. They were looking to me for assurance that life goes on beyond death because they knew I had been there.

I imagine most of them wanted to hear me say something like, "Your son has not died! He has just changed form. He is still with you, but he's now in the state of non-duality." Or perhaps they anticipated I would say, "We never die. Death is an illusion. He is happy and free! He wants you to be happy for him!"

I may even have received applause from the audience for saying something along those lines. But even though I *know* from my own experience that *all* of those statements are true, as I stood there watching the tears streaming down this woman's cheeks, those words would not come out of me. Any and all words simply rang hollow in my head, and it felt that I would be offering platitudes; just to say the "right thing" seemed condescending. Even though I have experienced the love and beauty of the other realm, as long as I remain in human form, I still feel pain. I still feel hurt. I still feel sorrow. In that moment, I felt strongly that it would have been disingenuous for me to try to tell her how she *should* feel and how she *should* handle such an unbearably painful situation.

Of course she is missing the physical presence of her only child, I thought. *She misses his smile, his voice, the feel of his skin, the texture of his hair, the sound of his laughter, his smell, and all his little ways.* I could sense that she was probably still having difficulty getting rid of his belongings and was probably even burying her face in his sweatshirt to try to fill the ragged hole in her heart. I know this because of all the stories about grieving for their loved ones that people have shared with me, hoping that I will give them some words of comfort to alleviate their pain.

Without thinking of the program or the people in the audience or anything else, I walked off the stage, down the steps, and toward this lovely lady, while at the same time motioning for her to come forward toward me. When we met, I put my arms around her and held her tight. In that moment, I did not know what else to do or say other than to connect with her physically, to show her that she was not alone.

"I am so sorry for your pain," I said, continuing to hug her. "I feel it as my own." As she cried into my shoulder, I could feel tears welling up within me, too. I could feel what she was feeling, all the sorrow and loss in her soul.

The emotions surrounding the woman's suffering didn't come only from the knowledge that she would never see her son on this physical plane again, but also from the strength of her will to live. I knew that in the grand scheme of things, if she were to die of a broken heart, she would be connected to him again and all would be well. But in that moment, the very human part of me did not want her to die of a broken heart. And I felt helpless. I knew that even with the knowledge gained from where I had been and what I had gone through, I could say nothing about my experience that would truly lift her grief right then and there. All I could do was hug her and let her cry—and assure her that her tears were the manifestation of the love she had for her son and her devotion to him. I wanted her to be safe in that knowledge—and to know that it was okay to feel pain.

After what could just as easily have been 1 minute or 10—I had no sense of time in that moment—we released each other from the hug and made eye contact. I didn't feel the need to say anything more, and so I slowly turned and walked back onto the stage, trying to regain my composure. It wasn't easy. I continued with the rest of my talk, but I struggled internally for the rest of the day, thankful when the event was finally over.

After I finished signing books and Danny and I were finally on our way back to our hotel, my husband turned toward me with a look of concern. "Are you okay?" Danny asked. "That woman's question about her son seemed to really get to you."

"Yes, I think I'm okay," I told him. "I'm just tired. I'll be fine by morning."

The Heart Has Its Reasons

When we got back to the hotel room, I kicked off my shoes and put the kettle on to make some tea. Then I relaxed into the armchair with my laptop to check my e-mail. I saw that my assistant had forwarded a message she had received just minutes ago via the "contact us" page on my website. The message, a very long one, was feedback from a woman named Shona who had been in the audience at the event earlier that day.

Shona wrote that when the grieving mother asked the question about her son, I should have assured her that her son was fine and that he continues to live in the other realm. I, of all people, should know that her son was not dead, Shona wrote, and I should have assured the lady that her son was happy, that life is an illusion, and that she should be happy for him. She went on at length to write out many of the truths I've shared in my first book and in my talks. Shona wanted to know why, when I had been given the perfect opportunity to say *all* these things that I'd said many times before and knew to be true from my NDE, I had not said *any* of them!

Shona wrote that she was very disappointed to see that I had gone backward in my teaching and that when presented with a real-life situation, instead of relying on what she knew I understood to be true, I had allowed myself to fall back into the illusion of suffering. My role was to uplift people and give them hope, she insisted, but instead I'd stooped to the level of those who were stuck in illusion.

My face was burning as I read the message—but not because I was angry with Shona. Far from it. I was upset because I felt I must have disappointed the rest of the audience as well. They'd wanted me to assure them about the bigger picture, and I had failed.

They'd expected me to raise their spirits, to give them something positive, and I had instead done the opposite.

Do Thoughts Create Reality?

That night, I tossed and turned in bed, replaying the events of the day. I started to tell myself that if I had disappointed the audience, perhaps it meant that they were perceiving me to be something that I am not. I have never tried to be an avatar or a guru, and my message has never been that we have to be positive at all times. In fact, I've always taught that thinking that way prevents us from truly allowing our authenticity to shine through. Believing that we have to be positive at all times also sends ourselves the message that who we are is not good enough, so we have to cover our true selves with a veneer of positivity.

My world was spinning. I started to ask myself, *Who would I be if I stopped giving people these messages? Who am I really? Who would I be if I disappointed people? Am I still as valuable to this world?*

Fear of disappointing others is one of the ways we lose ourselves and our authenticity. We try to meet the expectations of others instead of allowing ourselves to be who we are. I realized in that moment that even if I disappointed *everyone*, I could never go back to being the person I used to be—the people pleaser who danced for everyone else except myself. That was the person who gave and gave, even after I had nothing left to give myself, and then became so drained that I got cancer.

My mind went back to that time and the fear I felt at my lymphatic system being ravaged by cancer cells as the disease progressed in my body. I remembered how well-meaning people—those who had read all the spiritual books and completed all the self-improvement courses—would make pronouncements such as, "Your thoughts create your reality, and that means you must have created the cancer with your thoughts! So watch your thoughts!"

At first, I researched everything I could about the Law of Attraction because I wanted to defeat this beast that was ravaging my body. I wanted to understand how I had attracted it to me. So every time I had a thought I judged as negative, I nipped it in the bud, pushing it out of the way and burying it in the corners of my mind. But even so, the thoughts would resurface as the cancer continued to spread.

Fearing I wasn't being diligent enough, I became convinced I had to push myself and work harder at curtailing my negative thoughts. I created vision boards, cutting pictures out of magazines and pasting them onto poster board, and I visualized positive outcomes over and over. Every time a fearful thought about cancer or death would come into my mind, I became even *more* fearful, believing that each of these thoughts would directly contribute to the progression of my illness. So I tried to force myself not to think them!

Why am I still having negative thoughts? I would ask myself angrily. *I'm working so hard at controlling them and at being positive and creating a positive reality. Why is it still not working? Why is the cancer still progressing?*

The fear and frustration I felt during that time was palpable, and speaking with well-meaning people often only made me feel worse. I truly believed that the cancer was progressing because I was "not getting it." I was convinced that my beliefs weren't strong enough or that my thoughts weren't positive enough—or both.

The Full Experience of Being Human

Lying in bed that night, I tossed and turned for hours before finally falling asleep. When I woke up in the morning, I still felt exhausted—both from the full-day event I'd just finished as well as from being awake half the night. I'd overslept because of how late it was when I'd fallen asleep, and when Danny (who was already in the shower) heard me moving around, he reminded me that we had to hurry because we would soon be heading to the airport.

I found myself feeling really sluggish and slow that morning, still struggling to reconcile and integrate the events of the previous day. The thought occurred to me that no matter how many books we read, how deeply spiritual our experiences are, how awakened we think we have become, or how many people we teachers attract to our seminars, we cannot totally alleviate human suffering.

I'm certainly not saying that being spiritually aware isn't important. After all, the more aware we become of our connection to everyone and everything, the less likely we are to hurt others (in our own family and circle of friends, in our community, or in the greater world) and cause pain or to damage our environment or the planet. But deep pain is merely the other side of the same coin as deep love. Part and parcel of this human experience is feeling pain and hurt when someone we love dies. How could I explain to people that no matter how hard I try to describe the magnificence I experienced in the other realm—and no matter how much assurance I give that everything is actually perfect in the grand scheme of things—while we are here in this life, the feelings of pain, shame, disappointment, fear, suffering, and so on are still very real?

Allowing Yourself to Feel Pain

No matter how much we are convinced that we will wake up from this mortal illusion when we die, it doesn't necessarily diminish the agony of a newly widowed husband or a parent who has lost a child. Those who have experienced the trauma of losing family members to a tsunami, an earthquake, or a school shooting will undoubtedly go through grief and anguish. Those who are taking care of a family member with a serious or terminal illness will feel suffering, loss, and pain.

The hunger of the poor beggar child in India, holding her younger brother in her arms as she looks at me with the wide eyes of anticipation—her little hand outstretched as I pass by on the street—is real. No amount of convincing the hungry little girl that this is an illusion, and that it's all perfect in the grand scheme of things—all part of the yin and yang, the negative and the positive that make up this life of duality—will alleviate her (or her baby brother's) hunger.

So when I am faced with someone who is truly hurting, and they ask why their situation is so painful, I feel torn. I'm torn between giving them my take on why pain exists—as viewed from the perspective of the greater tapestry—and truly acknowledging and honoring that person's pain right where they are in that moment, allowing them to feel whatever they are feeling without judgment.

These days, when the popular belief seems to be that "a positive attitude creates a positive reality," those of us going through pain and anguish deal with more than just our own suffering. We also have to deal with the attitudes of those around us who insist we stay positive. While it's natural to feel some really hard emotions when dealing with pain and loss, a significant segment of our society feels uncomfortable with it. If we follow the supposedly enlightened way of thinking, we are discouraged from having an authentic experience. We are led to believe that if we feel pain, we are failing in some way.

Feeling optimism and hope are certainly beneficial, but when life's calamities inevitably befall us, believing that we need to stay positive through the crisis just adds to our burden. We then often feel ashamed of our pain, thinking we brought it on ourselves with our lack of spirituality. Likewise, when others are suffering, we don't honor the space for them to express their pain, instead offering platitudes and advice. But while positive thinking and affirmations are valuable in many ways, there are times when they're not helpful in the least! They can act like Band-Aids that simply cover a wound so we can't see it.

I've learned that the best way *out* of pain is to go *through* it. That's where the real gold lies. This means first recognizing that the pain's there, and then accepting it. You acknowledge its presence and allow yourself to truly feel it. You *own* it.

Pain is *never* without gifts. Above all else, pain gives us the empathy to better understand others who are also going through loss, grief, and suffering. These experiences actually make us more human—and more divine.

Just Be Yourself

During all that tossing and turning I'd done the previous night, I remembered some of the lessons I'd learned in my NDE. For one, I learned that my *negative thoughts* weren't what caused the cancer. My *lack of self-love* was responsible. To me, that lesson was pure gold, and it only came to me once I'd come through the other side of pain. True, I didn't *choose* to go through the pain—I resisted for as long as I could, trying to cover it up with positivity. But the gift came after I could no longer resist.

Prior to getting cancer, I'd spent a lifetime trying to be positive, always putting on a smiling face because I wanted to be liked. Whenever I felt a negative thought, I would quash it, never allowing people to see me as fearful.

So when my cancer showed up, I really could not understand how that could happen when I had always been such a positive person! I believed that my thoughts must have created the cancer, and so I would fear my thoughts. And then I also feared *the fear of* my thoughts. I was drowning in a never-ending whirlpool of fear! But in the NDE, I realized that the key wasn't *being positive,* it was *being myself*! I didn't need to eradicate all negative thoughts, I needed only to *love myself for who I am, not for who others wanted me to be*! If only I had known that truth, I would never have feared my thoughts, because I would have realized that my thoughts are part of who I am. Denying my negative emotions and believing that this negativity was wrong only exacerbated my problems.

Come from the Heart

So on that morning after I read the e-mail, when I was feeling sluggish and heavy, there I was once again—being dragged into a place of trying to be what someone else wanted me to be. Then Danny reminded me that we had to check out of the hotel soon, so I started getting dressed and packed the last of my bags. Not long after we went down to the lobby, someone called out to me from the other end of the room. I looked up to see a blonde-haired woman walking toward me, smiling. Introducing herself as Ariana, she said, "I was at your event yesterday, and I really enjoyed it. I learned *a lot!*"

"Thank you so much," I replied, not only glad but also relieved to hear she had enjoyed the workshop.

"I had one question, if you don't mind," she said.

"No, I don't mind at all," I told her. "Go ahead—what's your question?"

"I would love to do something similar to what you do," Ariana began. "I want to conduct workshops, speaking to people and inspiring them. What advice would you give me on the best way to truly inspire others?"

I rarely think about how I'm going to answer a question like that. Instead, I just say the first thing that comes into my head. It always seems to be exactly what the person needs to hear, and it was no different this time.

"Don't think in terms of inspiring other people," I told her. "Just follow your own heart, and do whatever it takes to inspire *yourself.* Then just share what you've learned. Your focus needs to be on *you*, not on the audience. As long as you are keeping yourself inspired and passionate about life, all you have to do is speak your own truth from your heart! That's it!"

"So I don't need to work at inspiring other people?" Ariana asked. "I just have to inspire myself and find things I believe in, things that I feel passionate about, and share these things from my heart?"

"Yep," I responded. "As soon as we *try* to inspire other people, or *try* to say what we think others want to hear or be who we think they want us to be, then we are no longer being authentic. We are coming from the head and not the heart. When we come from the heart instead, we allow the message to come *through* us, rather than *from* us.

"My core teaching is about the importance of being authentic above everything else. So when I am focused on trying to give the audience what I think they want, I end up doing the opposite of what I'm encouraging them to do. That's the dichotomy! Does that make sense?"

"Yes, very clearly!" Ariana said. "Thank you for your time!"

I barely heard her response, though, because all of a sudden, I realized that those very words I had just spoken to her were for *me*! They were the answers I needed to hear myself! I felt so light and energized from the brief but powerful experience that I barely noticed Ariana giving me a quick hug and then Danny urgently ushering me into the vehicle waiting outside to take us to the airport.

The tightness and constraint I'd felt earlier that morning disappeared. I felt freer, more alive . . . more relaxed. *I got it!* I didn't have to worry about the e-mail—or about anything! I had done the right thing the day before with the grieving mother because I'd followed what I felt in my heart, and that is the whole point of my message—to be yourself!

Once Danny and I returned home that evening, I checked my e-mails and discovered a message waiting for me from the beautiful woman who had lost her son. She thanked me for allowing her the space to feel her feelings, and she was especially grateful that I did not judge her grief or, even worse, dismiss her pain with trite sayings and advice. Her words made me smile from a place deep inside.

Experiences like this remind me of the risk of being an author and speaker in the field of self-help, inspiration, or spirituality: We can easily become trapped into making sure that we always show only our "best self" in public and come across as being "spiritually knowledgeable" and a spiritual authority. As a result, we can completely lose ourselves in trying to please or impress others.

I want to clarify that I am in no way dismissing the Law of Attraction, nor am I saying that keeping positive thoughts and attitudes is not helpful. What I *am* saying is that I believe we attract many of the events and situations in our lives not only by our thoughts and attitudes, *but also by who we are*! We attract that which is truly ours, that which we really need at any given time—both positive and negative.

This means that the more we love and value ourselves—and the more we naturally choose to live from a place of joy and feel we are worthy and deserving—the more our lives will reflect these emotions. This will take us to a state of feeling *optimistic*, which is a far healthier state than just trying to be positive.

In order to accomplish this, we must stop trying to feel or think a certain way and embrace all of our emotions, including all our disappointment, frustration, pain, sorrow, and grief—*without judgment*. We have to accept *all* these aspects of ourselves because *that* is where our deepest humanity lies.

Living Heaven *Here and Now*

If "We must always be positive" is a *myth*, then what could be the *truth*?

Consider These Possible Truths

- We can't control having negative thoughts, so trying to push them away doesn't make them disappear; at most, this just buries them temporarily.

- It's okay to feel pain, anger, sadness, frustration, fear, and so on. They're a natural part of who we are as human beings.

- Experiencing so-called negative emotions does not mean that we have failed or that we are not spiritual enough.

- Embracing pain gives us an opportunity to see its gifts (which can only appear once we arrive on the other side of the pain).

- Negative thoughts don't make us sick; not loving ourselves for who we truly are has a much greater affect on our health.

- When we love ourselves, it's easier to stay optimistic. Optimism is a far more powerful state than trying to be "positive" because it comes from a deeper place of self-love.

- We attract events and circumstances in our lives not based solely on our thoughts and attitudes but on who we are and how well we accept and express that.

Tips and Exercises

- Realize that having negative thoughts doesn't mean you are a negative person or that you are causing yourself harm—it means you are human.

- When you feel fear and negativity, don't fight the feelings or judge yourself for having them. Instead, allow yourself to acknowledge these emotions and feel them fully so you can move through them without getting stuck.

- Learn to love yourself and feel deserving of joy so you will be able to feel it naturally (instead of trying to force joy, which is impossible).

- If you are having difficulty getting to a place of joy, start with acceptance for where you are right now. After acceptance, reach for finding peace with your current situation. From peace, it becomes easier to step into a place of gratitude, and from gratitude you can more easily get to joy. Joy comes as a result of having extreme gratitude and appreciation for the state of our lives in the present moment.

- Look back on some past painful experiences, and try to identify some things you gained—both large and small—from these experiences. Feel grateful for these gifts.

- Allow others to feel whatever they may be feeling, having compassion for what they are experiencing without judging them for it.

Questions to Ask Yourself

- Am I coming from my heart in expressing my truth, or do I get stuck in my head, trying to figure out who I think I am supposed to be to fit in or please others?

- Does it feel safe to experience negative emotions? If not, what do I need to do to allow myself to feel safe in expressing who I truly am?

- When I am judging my thoughts or actions, what fear is behind that judgment? What would it feel like to let that judgment go?

- Can I honor another's pain and allow them to be authentic without fearing that I am somehow buying into the illusion of duality?

I know I am accepting the entirety of who I am, including all my thoughts and feelings, when . . .

- I don't try to push away negative thoughts but instead allow myself to acknowledge them and feel them fully whenever they crop up.

- I don't concern myself with what others may want me to think and feel; I love and accept all my emotions as a part of who I am—with no judgment.

- I am able to express my true self by connecting with what makes me feel the most joy and passion.

AFTERWORD

Just as I was completing the final chapters of this book, I received the shocking news that my dear friend Dr. Wayne Dyer had passed away.

Shortly before this news arrived, a few close friends had come over to have lunch with Danny and me at our new home in California. When my friend Jennifer McLean arrived, she was bearing a huge bouquet of orange roses.

"What's with the orange?" she asked as she handed me the armful of flowers.

"What do you mean?" I responded with a curious smile as I happily accepted her gift, admiring the striking color and reveling in the sweet scent. They were absolutely stunning.

"While I was in the flower store, I was reaching for the red roses for you," Jennifer explained, "but I kept hearing this voice in my head saying, 'Get the orange ones. Get the *orange* ones!' You obviously have a friend on the other side who really wanted you to have the orange roses!"

"Well, orange *is* my favorite color," I said. "But I can't think of who from the other realm would have told you that." For a few moments, I worried that someone close to me might have passed away without me knowing and was trying to send me a message. But I soon got busy with the final preparations for lunch and forgot about my apprehension.

Shortly after, while we were sitting down to eat, my cell phone rang. When I looked at the caller ID, I saw that it was Maya Labos, who had been Wayne's personal manager and right hand for the last 38 years. Because she travels with him on every trip, Maya and I have gotten extremely close since I'd been sharing the stage with Wayne for the past few years.

"Maya! What's up?" I asked cheerfully as I answered the call.

"It's Wayne," came the tearful voice, and I already knew what was coming next. "He died in his sleep this morning. He's gone."

With those words, my heart sank to the pit of my stomach. I just couldn't believe it was true. Wayne Dyer could not possibly be dead! I had just finished a speaking tour of Australia with him the week before, and he'd seemed positively pulsing with life—as always!

Then I remembered my earlier hunch that someone had crossed over, and I realized my premonition had been true after all. Wayne had known that orange was my favorite color. He often teased me backstage about my penchant for orange (my wallet, my phone case, and my purse are all orange). And he too had a thing for oranges—the fruit, that is. He always carried an orange onstage as a prop when explaining one of his famous analogies. Wayne was rarely, if ever, onstage without an orange, and he'd often toss it into the audience when he finished making his point.

In fact, his teaching about the orange was the last post made on his Facebook page before he died: "When you squeeze an orange, you'll always get orange juice to come out. What comes out is what's inside. The same logic applies to you: When someone squeezes you, puts pressure on you, or says something unflattering or critical, and out of you comes anger, hatred, bitterness, tension, depression, or anxiety, that is what's inside. If love and joy are what you want to give and receive, change your life by changing what's inside."

I knew that giving the message to my friend Jennifer to get the orange roses was Wayne's way of saying that he's fine. And although I knew, probably better than most, that Wayne was having a grand time where he was now—laughing and dancing in pure joy, bathed in the overwhelming feelings of unconditional love, free from pain, free from expectations, free to expand and transcend—I was still stunned and saddened.

Wayne had been my teacher, my mentor, and one of my biggest cheerleaders in the journey that he had invited me to begin as an author and a speaker. If he hadn't discovered my story on the Internet and then told Hay House to track me down and invite me to write a book about my experience, I would not be a published author today, traveling the world, sharing my insights onstage, and seeing my life being made into a Hollywood movie!

While on tour at Hay House events, Wayne and I had often talked about the afterlife and the expansion that takes place once we leave the physical body. Now, I couldn't help but smile as I imagined him experiencing this for himself firsthand.

Wayne is, and always was, a passionate teacher. That's what he was put on this earth to do—to teach. And I doubt that shedding his body has stopped him. If anything, he's even more passionate because now he can reach more people, all at once! He's probably teaching in a far greater and grander way than he had ever hoped to accomplish while in the physical realm! Instead of being gone for good, he is now more accessible to the millions of people who love him, and he's probably having a blast showing up in different creative ways for all the people he's touched in some manner. Now that he is no longer restricted by the physical, Wayne is here, there, and everywhere!

One day, we will all transcend this physical plane into the infinite realm of the afterlife, and while many fear what lies beyond, crossing over is actually the easy part. Let me assure you that there is nothing to fear beyond the veil. Our true challenge is in trying to live a life of expansion, liberation, love, and joy *here* on the physical plane.

So my biggest message (inspired by both my NDE and the life and teachings of my dear friend) is to live your life as an exercise in creativity, as if every discovery, every artistic exploration, matters in the cosmic tapestry of life—*because it does*. Follow your heart as you exuberantly combine the riot of colors the universe lays before you to make your life into your own masterpiece. You may be surprised by your creation. As when we listen to or play beautiful music, our goal is not to get to the end of the piece. The point is to enjoy the melodious, joyous journey the music takes us on, including the very first note and every single one that comes after it. And as Wayne always said, "Don't die with your music still in you!"

So don't be afraid of not doing it right or of not being good enough. Such fear is totally unfounded. Life is not about getting it right, figuring out the answers to the really big questions (or even the small questions, for that matter), reading all the right books, taking all the right courses, or studying with the masters. Nor is it about whether you've had deep spiritual experiences, achieved altered states of consciousness, or become a spiritual guru to multitudes. It's not even about whether you've been dead and come back to life to share your experiences—trust me!

The *only* thing that matters is that you allow yourself to be all of who you are! It's that simple! *Just be yourself*—your *true* self! Be the *love* that you are. Shine your light as brightly as you can. And while you're at it, don't forget to enjoy the ride and have fun— *lots* of fun!

Wayne is now perfectly cognizant of the artistry of his life and of all the millions of people who have been touched with the brush of his mastery. Thank you, my friend, for coming into our lives and for sharing your beauty, wisdom, and humor with us as we make this journey together—and *thank you* for the orange roses.

Namaste

ACKNOWLEDGMENTS

For me, this is one of the most important parts of this book. It's where I get to express my gratitude to everyone who, in some way or another, has been an integral part of my journey and who was involved—either directly or indirectly—in bringing this book into being.

First and foremost, I'd like to thank my best friend and soul brother, Rio Cruz. Whatever I say in gratitude sounds trite and doesn't even come close to how I feel about your support in encouraging me to give voice to my message. During the years, you've played such an integral part in my journey in so many ways. Your unyielding conviction in my testimony kept me going when others challenged me. Thank you for being my greatest cheerleader and my sounding board, as well as for helping me to stay sane as I tried to fit into a world that wasn't always ready to hear what I had to share. Thank you, my friend. I love you dearly.

To my close friend and confidant Maya Labos: Thank you for being my soft place to land when we are on the road and for being my surrogate family member. You are my "go to" person for all things related to the world of public speaking and beyond. Thank you for being there through the ups and downs of this speaking journey, for being my partner in crime and all-round fun person to travel with during speaking events, and for being my pillar of strength through the death of our dear friend Dr. Wayne Dyer.

To my amazing editor, Katy Koontz: Thank you so much for being such a beautiful light, and for being so easy to work with and for making this project effortless for me! You are an angel, and I am so grateful for your astute understanding of what I was always trying to say.

To Patty Gift from Hay House: Thank you for being such a delight to work with! I have truly been touched and honored by your support and interest in my work. Thank you!

To Tina Kapadia and her beautiful family, who welcomed both Danny and me into their hearts and their home. Thank you for your generosity and for sharing your lives with us, and for making us feel at home in a foreign land.

To my dear friend Jason Garner and his lovely wife, Christy, who extended their home to Danny and me as we straddled two continents: Thank you not only for your hospitality, but also for all the stimulating conversations and fireside chats. I'm looking forward to more!

To my wonderful superteam, who are nothing short of angels. They are the ones who work with me behind the scenes, keeping all the cogs and gears running, going above and beyond the call of duty: First, thank you to my two amazing assistants, Roz Brooks and Milena Joy Morris; and also special thanks to Rita Pape, Ted Slipchinsky, Kathi Blinn, Loreto Torres, Tammy Holmes Short, Angelika Farrell, Sandra Gee, Ravinder Basi, Rick Burr, Richard Machin, and Sandy Shriver. Thanks to every single one of you for all you have done and continue to do to keep the wheels turning.

To my dear friend Renu Malani: Thank you for making all my visits home amazingly bright with your laughter and wit, and for being a co-conspirator on my journey to prove that "enlightenment" can be attained via humor, fun, and chocolate! I love you, buddy.

To my beautiful family: my brother, Anoop, who means the world to me (more than words can describe); his family, Mona and Shahn; my dear mother, whose love for me has always been unwavering and unconditional; and my wonderful father-in-law, whose support has meant so much to me. Last but not least, thanks to my darling husband, Danny. It has been a joy to share this world, this time-space reality, and this existence with you. I'm so blessed to have you in my life and love you to eternity and back. You are the reason behind everything I do, the wind beneath my wings.

This section would not be complete without giving a heartfelt thanks to dear Wayne Dyer. No words can express the gratitude I feel for you, Wayne, for sharing your platform and for bringing me into the public arena. Without you and the divine intervention that brought us together, this book would not exist, and I would possibly not be doing what I'm currently doing. Thank you for being my beacon and for bringing me onto the most perfect path—even before I knew that this was what I was meant to do! I know you can hear me and that you continue to guide me from the other realm. I love you, my friend.

I'd also like to thank every single one of *you* who are holding this book in your hands as well as those of you who wrote to me after reading my first book. Thank you for all your support, your letters, and your outpouring of love. Without you, I wouldn't be doing what I am doing today. Watch out! I can already feel another book coming on!